13.7/2017.9/17

TRYING TO FLOAT

*Coming of Age
in the Chelsea Hotel*

NICOLAIA RIPS

SCRIBNER
New York   London   Toronto   Sydney   New Delhi

Scribner
An Imprint of Simon & Schuster, Inc.
1230 Avenue of the Americas
New York, NY 10020

This book weaves together what the author experienced, what she was told, and what she imagined. Many names and identifying characteristics have been changed.

First Scribner hardcover edition July 2016

SCRIBNER and design are registered trademarks of The Gale Group, Inc., used under license by Simon & Schuster, Inc., the publisher of this work.

For information about special discounts for bulk purchases, please contact Simon & Schuster Special Sales at 1-866-506-1949 or business@simonandschuster.com.

The Simon & Schuster Speakers Bureau can bring authors to your live event. For more information or to book an event, contact the Simon & Schuster Speakers Bureau at 1-866-248-3049 or visit our website at www.simonspeakers.com.

Interior design by Jill Putorti

Manufactured in the United States of America

10 9 8 7 6 5 4 3 2 1

Library of Congress Cataloging-in-Publication Data

Names: Rips, Nicolaia, author.
Title: Trying to float : coming of age in the Chelsea Hotel / Nicolaia Rips.
Description: First Scribner hardcover edition. | New York : Scribner, 2016.
Identifiers: LCCN 2016014365| ISBN 9781501132988 (hardcover) | ISBN 9781501133008 (ebook)
Subjects: LCSH: Rips, Nicolaia—Childhood and youth. | Coming of age—New York (State)—New York. | Girls—New York (State)—New York—Biography. | Teenage girls—New York (State)—New York—Biography. | Chelsea Hotel Biography. | New York (N.Y.)—Biography. | Bohemianism—New York (State) New York. | Eccentrics and eccentricities—New York (State)—New York. | New York (N.Y.)—Social life and customs. | BISAC: BIOGRAPHY & AUTO-BIOGRAPHY / Personal Memoirs. | BIOGRAPHY & AUTOBIOGRAPHY / Literary. | BIOGRAPHY & AUTOBIOGRAPHY / Women.
Classification: LCC F128.57.R57 A3 2016 | DDC 974.7—dc23 LC record available at https://lccn.loc.gov/2016014365

ISBN 978-1-5011-3298-8
ISBN 978-1-5011-3300-8 (ebook)

To Michael, Sheila, and everyone else
who gave me something to complain about

Practically everybody in New York
has half a mind to write a book, and does.

—GROUCHO MARX

TRYING
TO FLOAT

CONTENTS

CONTENTS

PROLOGUE

IT WAS 11:00 p.m. on the Saturday night just before Christmas, and I had been sent out by my parents to buy ice cream from the nearby Aristocrat Deli. As I waited for the elevator, I amused myself with a favorite activity: seeing how far I could pull the clasp on the ancient fire alarm without breaking its tiny glass tube.

But that night, my chubby seven-year-old fingers slipped, and I clamped down hard on the lever.

The fire alarms exploded through the hallways, and I kicked the pieces of glass behind a nearby garbage can. Neighbors swelled from their apartments; they carried guitars, guns, furs, paintings, and manuscripts, labored under mannequins and giant antique cameras. They yelled and grumbled, rubbed sleep from their eyes, and jostled each other, angry at having been forced out of their snuggeries. My mother, in a nightgown, picked me up in a one-arm hold that would shame a running back, and raced us down the hotel's peeling iron staircase. In her other arm was a stack of brightly painted journals that documented her thirty years of travels through Asia, Africa, and the Middle East. Spices and flora she had dried and pressed in them escaped in a puff of fragrance as we ran. My father, trailing behind us in a mink-lined smoking jacket, cradled a bottle of gin.

In the lobby, we were greeted by a crowd of men and women in silk dressing gowns, with smudged eyeliner and wigs awry, and in the middle of them, The Angel—naked but for a white cloth wrapped around his groin and a luminous spread of feathers attached to his back.

With no chance of returning to our rooms until firemen had canvassed the ten-story building, the mood in the lobby turned from communal annoyance to collective intoxication (drinks courtesy of my father's bottle of gin and El Quijote, the ancient Spanish restaurant next door). People milled about, catching up with neighbors.

Relieved that I had not yet been arrested (which is not to say that others weren't that night), I walked outside. It was snowing. Not white flakes. Rose flakes—steeped in the dozen red letters that hung over the front door: HOTEL CHELSEA.

THE
FLEDGLING
YEARS

MY FIRST TRIP

EIGHT YEARS INTO my parents' marriage, my mom discovered that she was pregnant. This seemingly joyous event was dented by my dad's denial that such a terrible thing could happen to him. Convinced that he wasn't responsible, he accused my openly gay godfather, Tom, of fathering the child.

My mom was an extraordinary traveler, and though excited about the pregnancy, feared that a baby would signal the end of her journeys. She began to plan a trip to Iran.

Because she needed a visa to get into Iran and couldn't get one in the United States, she flew to London and applied for her visa there. She was five months pregnant.

In London, the Iranian consulate informed her that a visa could take months. Never one to wait around, she decided to travel the Uzbek silk road while waiting for her visa to arrive in Tashkent. An Iranian doctor in London gave her a note that said she could travel until seven months pregnant. With this, she and I were off.

Back in New York, my dad refused to admit that he had a wife, much less a daughter on the way. This fantasy came to an end when he picked up his mail to find a postcard from a grinning woman, with a swelling belly, firing off automatic weapons with a group of equally happy Uzbek men. The caption read, "Enjoying the afternoon with your daughter!"

Acknowledging the imminent arrival of his daughter, my father, who had previously handled my mother's trips to the most dangerous parts of the world by confining himself to a two-block radius that included the Chelsea Hotel, his favorite café, and his barber, now added visits to a psychiatrist to the mix. What she thought of his reflections on his childhood in Nebraska, vivid and unexpected, like pimentos in the center of olives, I dare not imagine.

On July 19, exactly four weeks before I was born, my father opened the door to find a woman wearing a burka. When my mother went into labor at St. Luke's–Roosevelt Hospital, my dad was finally forced to venture outside his circle of comfort. Having done so—and meeting me—he realized it wasn't so bad out there.

ITALY

MOTHER LOOKED AT Father, Father at Mother, both at me (in my crib), and they decided that the best thing for the three of us was to move to Italy.

To this day I do not understand why, but I spent the next couple years crawling around a small town north of Rome called Sutri, while my mother painted and my father did God knows what. Mostly, he sat with the old men in the square. He spoke no Italian, relying instead on an array of confusing facial expressions.

After Italy, we moved to North Africa and then to India. We lived in villages. My babysitters there didn't know the few words I'd learned in Italy, so I became fluent in the same language of baffling facial expressions as my father.

When we finally returned to the United States, we moved back to the Chelsea Hotel, known for its writers, artists, and musicians, but also for its drug addicts, alcoholics, and eccentrics. At any given time, at least one from each group was in the lobby. Since there were few children in the hotel, it was with these people that I spent my time.

PRESCHOOL

MY EARLIEST MEMORIES of my father are of him sitting in an armchair, me on his lap, reading to me from various books. Instead of the stories with which you and I are so familiar and fond (*Charlotte's Web, The Little Prince*), he would convert whatever he was currently reading into a children's story.

I suspect he did this not because he was lazy, which he most certainly was, but because he liked the challenge of turning *The Idiot* or anything by Thomas Carlyle, his favorite, into a tale for five and under.

This would have been harmless enough had he not believed that reading adult books to a child—followed by a discussion—was a more effective means of developing his daughter's mind than any of the usual methods.

There were two effects of this (noticeable to everyone but my father): the reading and chatting continued well past when other parents began to teach their children to read; and the language of Carlyle began to seep into the soft brain of his child (me).

After reading to me for a couple hours, my father would pack me up and take me to his favorite coffee shop on Eighth Avenue. The Big Cup was brightly painted, filled with broken chairs and sofas, and, to my delight, had Barbie dolls nailed to the doors of the bathrooms. The dolls, mostly Kens, were naked.

The coffee shop was popular with young men who looked like Ken and older men who wanted to meet young men who looked like Ken. I was the only child there, and as one of the first regular customers, I became a sort of mascot.

———

By the time I was four and it had occurred to my parents that I should be in preschool, the schools near the Chelsea Hotel were full. So my parents put my name on waiting lists (with my father placing asterisks next to those schools closest to his favorite coffee shops), but there was little hope. In the meantime, I passed my days in the hotel lobby and The Big Cup, talking to the residents and regulars.

One day my parents received a call from a school in the neighborhood. A spot had opened up, but because there were others on the waiting list, the head of the school wanted to interview us all before deciding who would be admitted.

Though a foreign concept to me at the time, parents in Manhattan are beset with the school system, believing that the right preschool is essential to getting their kid into the right elementary school, middle school, high school, college, and so on. The competition is so great that parents pay people to prepare their families for the interviews. The coaches go so far as to pick out the clothing the family will wear.

The school that called my parents was on West Fourteenth Street in an area called the Meatpacking District. It was once a center for butchering meat and is now filled with fancy shops. Because of the school's reputation as creative and safe, it was attended by the sons and daughters of famous actors and actresses who lived in the neighborhood. So well known was the school that the headmistress was a neighborhood celebrity, fawned over by conniving parents.

Upon entering the school, my parents and I were escorted into a waiting room. The headmistress, we were told, would be with us in a few minutes.

Also in the room were another mother, father, and a young boy. The child was wearing khaki pants, a blazer, and a tie.

I was wearing my favorite skirt and top, made of a bright, shimmery fabric which my mom had bought for me in Morocco. Since the outfit was several years old, the top was no longer within sight of the skirt, and the skirt was much tighter and shorter than it was meant to be. There was a matching headscarf.

The secretary instructed me and the other child to take a seat next to each other on the couch. Sitting there, he in his khakis and blazer and me in my ensemble, we gave the appearance of a psychiatrist and his patient, who, six months after Halloween, was still wearing her genie costume.

What's more, after a few seconds of pointed whispering, the other parents explained that this was *their* interview, not ours, and that if we wished not to embarrass ourselves, we should leave before the headmistress arrived.

Not a chance, replied my mother. They were the ones who had it wrong.

As long as I had known my mother and father, they had not once been in the right place at the right time. So I was surprised to see my mother reach into her pocket and pull out a calendar, with which she intended to demonstrate that these people had made the mistake.

There was no time to settle this. The headmistress had arrived.

Surprised to see two families at the interview, she announced that there was clearly a mix-up, but no matter. She would be happy to interview the two children together.

She may have been happy, but the boy's parents were not. My mother, on the other hand, had not heard any of it; having arrived at the relevant dates in her calendar, she realized that she, her husband, and her daughter were precisely one week early to the appointment.

The headmistress began by asking the boy's parents to describe their son. What they said shocked me.

The young gent, Ethan, could not only read (I, as you know, wasn't close to it), but he was nearly fluent in a second language and was, according to his parents, beginning to read picture books in Greek. Ethan's parents assured the headmistress that they didn't think it necessary for their son to learn Greek, but that he had insisted. With this, Ethan tossed a smirk in my direction.

But that was not the amazing part. What knocked me out was this: no matter what Ethan's father or mother said about Ethan (great personality, athletic, two languages and ancient Greek), nothing seemed to impress the headmistress.

I was sunk. America was obviously stuffed with superinfants, against whom I could never measure up and in whose shadows I would spend the rest of my life.

There was only one hope. I glanced at Ethan's khakis for the familiar bulge of Huggies Little Movers.

I'd overheard Mom tell someone that the most important thing for any preschool interview was to make certain the school knew that your kid was toilet trained. Schools were, according to Mom, more likely to admit an idiot with bowel control than a little genius who needed to have his diapers changed.

For me, there was no possibility of going *sans* diaper to the interview. I hadn't yet graduated to the toilet and couldn't imagine being without protection at such an important appointment. Mom, though, had made sure my diaper was expertly hidden under my genie skirt.

But no luck. Ethan's khakis were bulgeless. In between his tutorials in ancient Greek, he had learned to control his sphincter.

After Ethan's father had concluded his recitation of Ethan's accomplishments, the headmistress turned to my parents and asked them, with not a hint of interest, what they thought I could add to the school.

It was my father who responded.

"To be honest, not much."

Traitor!

My mother touched his arm, but there was no stopping him.

"She is hard to understand—even to those who love her; she can't follow the illustrations in picture books, much less learn all twenty-six letters of the alphabet; she isn't athletic and is getting chubby; and, between us, she doesn't have any friends."

The headmistress stared at him.

"But there is one thing . . ."

Good God.

"If you need someone to deliver an after-dinner toast, there is none better—at least in her age group."

And what he said was true: I couldn't read, wasn't athletic, and didn't have friends, but there had been no shortage of dinner parties in whatever part of the world we had been living, and I'd heard enough people stand up and speak that I'd gotten the hang of it.

To this day, I'm not sure what caused my father to say what he did to the headmistress. My guess is that he sensed that she, despite her upright manner, was no stranger to the liquor cabinet and had probably spent more than a few hours throwing back drinks with her friends while entertaining them with stories about the school. She may have been amused at the idea of having a toddler who could perform a passable toast after milk and cookies.

To clinch the deal, and to my parents' amazement, I turned to the headmistress.

"Where is the ladies' room?"

What I would do there, I had no idea.

The next day I was admitted.

THE POOL PARTY

A WEEK OR so before preschool began, my mom announced that she knew a couple whose daughter would be attending the same school. A few days later we were off to dinner at the couple's house.

While I was happy to meet someone new, I wasn't optimistic. I did not do terribly well with kids. I spent most of my time with my parents and their contemporaries, which made me sound overly pompous to those my age. To be honest, I didn't have any friends, let alone a good one.

The couple's daughter, Greta, was smart and pretty (saucer-sized brown eyes; thick, ringleted hair), and to my surprise, we got along. She lived just around the corner from me, so I imagined that if we became close, there would be plenty of afternoons together.

On the first day of school, we sat cross-legged on the floor, holding hands. Soon, I was spending time with her friends.

For the first time in my life, I was not only getting to know a group of kids my own age but they seemed to like me.

Toward the end of the school year, Greta's family invited my family to the forty-fifth birthday of Greta's father at their country house in rural New York. Because the party was over the summer, there was going to be a piñata, an ice cream truck, a swimming pool, the whole bucket. And to think that all this was for a forty-four-year-old man turning forty-five. But I wasn't complaining.

The party started out well. Greta and I played, and I met all her cousins. Greta's chums from school were also there.

Having played with the other kids, whacked at the piñata, and taken a few to the head in the kids' volleyball game, I went over to the side of the pool to cool off. There I found Greta's aunt spraying sun lotion on her baby, Lola.

Lola's mother took the opportunity of my arrival to jump into the pool and swim to where her companions were having cocktails.

After a while, she returned to the spot where Lola and I were playing, and asked if I would hand Lola down to her in the pool. Excited to carry the baby, I agreed.

Reflecting back on this, it was clearly all the mother's fault. How else, after all, could I sleep at night?

I picked up Lola, wobbled a little this way, a little that way, and then, knowing that I was going down, lunged toward the pool. Lola's mom got more than Lola. The baby and I plunged down on top of Lola's mom, knocking her unconscious.

We all started to sink: Lola (a baby), myself (a five-year-old, who, due to the good-natured negligence of her parents, did not know how to swim), and a forty-year-old woman, who, owing to a few cocktails and a blow to the head, dropped quickly to the bottom of the pool, all the while dreaming of a beach in Tahiti with someone other than her husband.

Maybe the drowning of an infant would have gone without much notice, but certainly not an infant, a child, and a middle-aged woman. No, it was too much—plus the gasping and splashing and crying.

The party ran to the pool, shouting all sorts of things.

I would like to report that I heroically forced the baby's head above water before dragging baby and mother to shore, all to the amazement of the family and their guests, but this is not what happened.

It went more like this:

After struggling to keep my head afloat (by, yes, standing on the baby), I shouted at the crowd: "IT'S A BABY! IT CAN FLOAT! SAVE ME."

The crowd reeled the infant out of the pool and then hauled her mother up onto the cement, where one of the guests performed mouth-to-mouth. Soon, Lola's mother began to make low moaning noises, suggesting that she was still in Tahiti.

With Lola and her mother saved, the crowd discussed leaving me to drown, but their goodness won out, and I was pulled from the water.

Greta's father, the man whose birthday party I had ruined,

is a good and generous man, who showed no sign of holding the incident against me. Not so Lola's mom. And especially not so Greta.

I had humiliated her, ended her father's party before she could bring out the birthday cake, which she had spent all day baking, and, of course, I nearly drowned her infant cousin and beloved aunt.

Shortly after the party, Greta intimated that I was no longer her best friend (who could blame her), or even her friend (ditto), and that her new best friend was Anastasia ("Ana") Penny. But this was not the end of it, for Greta would become (as we climbed through school together) someone whom everyone liked and wanted to be with. And if there was one thing which Greta made known to everyone, it was that there was no place in the tribe of Greta for me, the drowner of infants.

THE CRAFTIES

WITH NO FRIENDS, I returned to spending my afternoons in the lobby of the hotel.

It probably hadn't changed since the building was built in 1884. The walls and high ceilings were a mustard-yellow color and were lined with paintings by residents and former residents. On one wall hung a Joe Andoe painting of a white-and-gray horse. Swinging above the brown-and-white marbled floors was an obese pink woman on a swing, her plump legs dangling mischievously, inviting us into the world beneath her legs.

The greatest thing about the lobby was that you were never alone. Residents and guests continuously buzzed in and out, as did starstruck visitors who would show up to take pictures of the famous and outrageous. Perhaps the residents gathered in the lobby to take a break from their small rooms (many were without bathrooms). Or perhaps they gathered because it was the only place in the hotel with Wi-Fi.

One of the first people I met in the lobby was an attractive

man in his forties. He had recently moved to New York from Paris, where he had lived for many years, taking photographs for fashion magazines. He was charming, with graying hair and a sharp jaw.

By chance, my mother knew him from Paris, where she'd lived and worked as a model in the 1980s. Now they had both given up their jobs in fashion and were painting in the Chelsea Hotel.

Shortly after my mom's friend moved to the Chelsea, he was followed by someone he had known since childhood. The friend wrote brilliant stories, and the two of them would sit in armchairs, talking, arguing, and insulting each other. Their conversations soon drew others.

Once, when my mom's friend, the painter, referred to the screenplay writer as "Mr. Crafty," the writer responded that the painter was much worse—"Uber-Crafty." As two others took sides in this debate, they were given names: "Crafty Number One" and "Crafty Number Two."

Mr. Crafty, the writer, had a pointy beard and glasses with thick black frames and blue lenses. Everything he did was slow and deliberate. Next to him was his wooden cane.

Mr. Crafty was also partially paralyzed owing to a stroke, which had left him, for two days, hallucinating facedown on the floor of his room in the hotel. He would have died there had he not been discovered by a bellhop—a story which he told often.

By the time I arrived at the Chelsea, the story had stretched:

Mr. Crafty was including other people's stories as if they were his own, the joints between them so expertly welded that it was impossible to tell whether it was Mr. Crafty who had fought his way out of Cambodia or the fellow on the ninth floor; whether it was Mr. Crafty who played with the Vienna Philharmonic or the woman whose picture he had seen in the paper that morning.

No one complained about this because everyone understood that the stroke had dried up Mr. Crafty's memory and that by repeating his story, however distorted, he was watering it back to life.

Without fail, the Crafties reclined in the tired chairs of the lobby each day. In my mind, I was "Little Crafty," the junior addition to their team, and they didn't care about my past as a baby drowner just as I didn't care about their own damaged histories.

HALLOWEEN

SOME OF MY favorite memories of the Chelsea Hotel are of Halloween.

People in the Chelsea spent months assembling their costumes. Because there were designers, dressmakers, and actors in the hotel, the daily outfits of the residents were colorful—a young Asian man, for example, regularly walked the halls with large wings glued to his back, multicolored makeup, and what could best be described as a Victorian-era diaper. Halloween took things to a whole new level.

My godfather, Tom, a hearty man of six feet two with thick graying hair, would make my costumes with all the mastery of a professional tailor. As my parents would nurse their post-party hangovers on November 1, Tom and I would sit in my tiny bedroom plotting next year's costume. We would spend the year designing costumes that were original, scary, and, as I got older, pretty. In October, my mom would enter the picture, using the makeup and hair skills she had developed as a model to transform me.

When I was in first grade, I decided to dress as my idol, Groucho Marx. I wore one of my dad's old suits, which Tom tailored to fit me, and my mom slicked back my hair with gel and painted on thick eyebrows and a mustache. The Marx Brothers were introduced to me through a boxed set found in the Chelsea Flea Market. Neither of my parents believed in cable (similar to others not believing in the moon landing), but they did own an ancient TV and VCR player. I would sit for hours in front of the TV watching tapes of Lucille Ball, Fred Astaire and Ginger Rodgers, Abbott and Costello, and, of course, Groucho Marx. As a present, my parents took me to visit the house where Groucho lived in L.A. (they were tearing it down when we arrived) and a bar where Groucho drank (my dad's idea). My obsession with Groucho blossomed when I discovered that he had passed away on my birthday. I comforted (and flattered) myself with the thought that his soul had wandered for years until finally coming down, on the anniversary of his death, into the body of a little girl, me.

In the days leading up to Halloween, the relative normal of everyday life was abandoned. In preparation for the many themed parties thrown each year—Dead Royals, Silent Screen Stars, and the Circus—hemlines grew shorter, haircuts choppier, and makeup wilder. The hotel was abuzz, a feeling that for one night of the year its residents would be praised for what had typically isolated them.

Hotel residents would leave their names with the front desk if it was okay for the children of the building to trick-or-treat at their door. At a designated time, kids would gather in the lobby and wait for a Chelsea employee to lead them through the building. The amount of candy we received fluctuated with the changing economic times, but it was usually bountiful.

On that Halloween, the hotel's residents were feeling particularly generous and our bag filled quickly. At one apartment, though, we knocked but no one answered. When we knocked harder, the door opened slowly.

The room was dark but for a small lamp in the corner. Beneath the lamp was a giant bowl of candy. We made our way across the apartment toward the Milk Duds, Mars bars, and Hershey Kisses. Halfway there, we noticed something sticky on our shoes.

We had stepped in a puddle of thick dark liquid. We stopped.

We then noticed that the liquid was dripping from above. Staring up, we saw a man—upside down, and hanging from the ceiling. His throat was slit.

We screamed.

His mouth dropped open into a toothy grin.

We ran back down the corridor.

There we passed an old woman who was sitting in a wheelchair. She was once a beautiful artist, who had very early success, but who'd lost control of herself. She lived in a tiny studio apartment crowded with every piece of artwork she had ever created. Every day a different personality popped up inside her. She would speak in a murmur. During the evening she sat outside her apartment, guarding the door, growling at those who passed. By the time my family moved into the Chelsea, she was on medication and would hold a lit flashlight beneath her face, as if to announce that after a long and terrible journey, she was back.

We called her Smiley.

On that Halloween, with the lights in the hotel dimmed and her head glowing from the beam of the flashlight, her face floated bodiless through the hallways.

MY STEED

A COUPLE OF weeks after Halloween I was sitting at home when there came a knock at the door.

"Who's there?"

"El Capitan!"

I opened the door.

There before me was a man in a white uniform, with gold buttons, silk braid, and white gloves. His hair was black, slicked back, and for a man in his fifties, he was striking, with a strong but jowly chin.

"Young lady of the house, since I have passed you in the hallways of this esteemed, though decrepit, inn but have not had the pleasure of introducing myself, allow me to now do so."

With that he began an exhausting list of his titles and offices which, but for the arrival of my mother, he would have continued until dusk.

"You are looking exceptionally handsome tonight, Capitan."

"I come directly from an affair at the consulate for His Majesty."

To all questions, the Capitan answered with either too many details (his list of titles, for example) or too few ("the consulate" and "His Majesty"), making it impossible to learn anything about him. He lived in an ornately furnished apartment on the eighth floor with an imposing, buxom woman whom he referred to as Lady Hammersmith.

———

The next night there was a knock on the door.

"Who's there?" I asked.

"Der Hauptmann!"

I recognized the voice.

"Capitan?"

"Ja, and Johnnie."

I opened the door. Before me was the largest, blackest, and most magnificent drooling beast I'd ever seen.

"I have come to take the lady of the house for a ride."

After climbing on the back of Johnnie (a Newfoundland), who was over twice my size, the Capitan led me around the Chelsea and then outside onto Twenty-third Street. At the end of our trip, the Capitan walked Johnnie and me into the Aristocrat Deli, where we dined on sorbet.

———

The Capitan was only one of many who would drop by our apartment for a meal, to look at my mother's art, to show off their own art, play a new song, or borrow money. Like the others, the Capitan would reciprocate by having us over to his place. We would walk up the stairs to the seventh floor and announce our arrival with the bull-shaped brass door knocker.

After a minute the Capitan would appear at the door in full nautical attire. With a flourish of his dehydrated hands, he would usher us into his one-bedroom apartment. He often told us to hurry to avoid the "evil stepsisters" that lived across the hall (Donald and Travis, interior decorators). Although stately, the Capitan was nearing mummification, since gin was the only liquid he drank. Mom described him as "self-pickled." My father described him as "well preserved."

The Capitan's home had the aura of an opium den. His bed was the centerpiece; a low rectangle with four wooden posts across which hung thick embroidered curtains and tapestries. Rugs and pillows in dark colors were scattered across the floor. Like his home, his meals were more elaborate than anyone else's in the Chelsea.

Cassoulets, Indonesian stews, and roasts of lamb and pork. Although I was too young to drink, I looked forward to the strange concoctions with which he greeted my parents. Stranger still were the Capitan's friends, who dressed in turbans, silk dressing gowns, and jewels. They would entertain me for hours with stories of life in foreign lands: Morocco, Mongolia, India, and New Jersey.

The most common meeting place in the hotel, however, was our home. The Capitan and his friends were as likely to drop by at midnight as they were in the afternoon. No matter when they arrived, they were always welcomed with a pitcher of gin.

———

My parents had moved into a one-bedroom in the Chelsea after they married. My father had studied at various prestigious universities well into his thirties. Arriving late to the concept of adulthood, he had decided that the most comfortable course of action would be to live in hotels. When my parents first met, my father was living at the Regency and my mother was living in an apartment she had bought with her modeling money. My father had a friend already living in the Chelsea Hotel, and the friend agreed to introduce them to the landlord, Stanley Bard. Stanley and my parents worked out a deal on a small apartment.

The apartment had old wood floors that had once been beautiful, and my mom's and her friends' artwork covered the walls. Before dinner parties my mom would get on all fours to hammer down the nails that had sprouted up through the floorboards from old age. There was also a nineteenth-century door from Morocco propped against the wall (to give the illusion of another room) and an Edwardian chaise longue from the Chelsea flea market. The paintings, furniture, food, and people resided harmoniously.

When my mother returned from Uzbekistan and it became

clear that I was going to need a place to sleep, my parents created a space for me in the living room, the size of a walk-in closet. Because the size of my room prevented me from having drawers, and because there was no closet within the closet, getting ready in the morning was a four-stage process:

First, to the bathroom, which meant going through my parents' room. Second, retrieve my undergarments from a cabinet in the living room. Then, back to my parents' bedroom for my clothes, and, finally, a search for shoes under my bed. I usually did this naked in the dark of the morning, but if by chance my parents were up, I would announce, "Avert your eyes," to which my dad would respond by politely looking away. My mom refused, claiming that having birthed me gave her the right to forgo such etiquette.

My room had one huge window that overlooked Chelsea and the Village. It fit my Victorian cast-iron bed, an antique wooden chest that I filled with books, and a leopard-print rug.

I was born in the year of the tiger and the month of the lion, so my mom decided that everything I wore should be feline-themed. I had tiger-print coats, leopard leggings, and lions dancing on my dresses.

Photographs and paintings by my mom and her friends adorned the walls. Above my door hung a painting by my father's friend Andre. Under his brush, the subject of each of his portraits morphed into the face of Andre himself. Since the painting above my door was of me, I looked like a five-year-old who had just been released from rehab.

My room was beautiful and homey. A carved wooden window, smuggled by my mother out of Yemen, allowed me to see into the kitchen, where my mom would whirl around creating meals, incorporating ingredients she had brought back from her trips abroad. No matter how many people dropped by, meals prepared in the tiny kitchen expanded miraculously. My mother loved her neighbors and because of this our apartment had joy.

In the living room was a wooden end table that, when company came, agreeably opened to accommodate the crowd. Dinner was always by candlelight. When sent to bed, I always left my door open a crack so the light could flood in and I could see the silhouettes of our guests laughing.

PIPPI

FROM THE EARLIEST I can remember, Mom sang to me. As soon as I could stand, she danced with me. Also, my godfather, Tom, who had a career in musical theater, and his boyfriend Jim, an opera singer, were often at our apartment, and would waltz with me through the hallways of the Chelsea. I had no idea what songs like "Is That All There Is?" or "Dulcinea" meant, but I knew the words and would sing them badly as I stumbled out of time.

So when I was told that my elementary school would begin each day with a dance class, I was thrilled.

It is certain that I had no talent, but I thought that I did, and, like many girls, dreamt of a career as a ballerina. My original plan was to be a jockey, but I grew tall and chubby, and was allergic to horses.

For the dance teacher to take me seriously, I would need a tutu and matching slippers. My parents indulged me.

As our teacher entered the room, she was exactly the person

I'd imagined—tall, with a thin, athletic body. Her strawberry hair was pulled into two braids, one hanging over each ear, and bangs that covered her forehead. She wore high stockings, a black leotard, and what looked like an apron. When Mom saw her, she mumbled, "Pippi Longstocking."

Surveying her new class, Pippi stopped when her eyes reached me.

Her face twisted.

She twirled a plait on a long finger.

"Tutus and slippers are not part of the dress code. And no pink," she spat.

My tutu was tightening.

"You," her eyes trained on me, "think that dance is about princesses, fairy godmothers, and hunky men . . ."

I hadn't considered that last one but was happy to include it.

"But for me and others, all of that is *passé*."

Pippi and others? *"Passé"?* The revolution was afoot and I was wearing the wrong shoes.

"For us," Pippi continued, "drunks stumbling around a bar is truer to dance than nutcrackers . . ."

Better tell my parents they have a future in dance.

As the weeks passed, Pippi led us through exercises aimed at drawing out our emotions. She would do this by putting on a song and asking us to express our feelings through movement, during which she would call out helpful instructions:

"Olivia, I really like your use of space; if only Nicolaia could do the same."

"Beautiful, Greta, the raw emotion in your spins is breath-taking."

"Wow, Uhura, something must have happened to you this weekend, this is powerful."

"Nicolaia, can you keep it down?"

"I didn't say anything!"

"I could hear you breathing."

"I want to express myself too."

"Okay, okay, just do it to the side. And try not to move your legs."

"Isn't that how you dance?"

"No, you're moving them excessively. No excessive leg movement. And try not to breathe so loud!"

I found it all very confusing because while there was "no wrong way to dance," Pippi assured us, I was never doing it right. If Pippi was correct and dancing was the essence of all of us, what did that mean about me? It took me many years to pinpoint the exact moment when I labeled myself as an outsider, but I think it began here.

Though Pippi was fond of "we," she was really only interested in the thin, athletic, and pretty "we," which excluded me, described by my mother, quite generously, as "solid."

It also excluded Doris, a classmate, who was short and mannish.

When Pippi asked each of us to dance so that she could get an idea of our talents, Doris displayed moves even more grating than mine: jerky thrusts of the arms interrupted periodically by strutting. Doris and I sat together during Pippi's dance class and came to know each other.

Doris was quiet (brought to this country from Brazil when she was seven, she was already well trained in the martial arts, the source of her dance moves), but there was a great deal going on inside her head.

Our conversations involved me making suggestions and her responding with facial expressions.

"Doris, are you thinking bad thoughts about Pippi?"

A smile.

"Does it involve a gun?"

A shake of the head, no.

"Rope?"

Another shake.

"Fire?"

A nod yes.

"You'd like to set Pippi on fire and push her out on stage in front of the parents and principal?"

A smile from Doris.

I tried to convince Doris that Pippi wasn't trying to be mean. Pippi just had a passion for dance and an idea of what it should look like, and she couldn't bring herself to foul it up with me in my tutu and Doris, the stomping pyromaniac.

Another thing about Pippi was that she made sure to include her own children in every performance. So the group numbers were filled exclusively with Pippi's daughter and son (both of whom attended the school), the thin girls in the class,

Uhura (my first crush), and a girl named Zalle, who was the only one among us who could actually dance.

Every day I took my place with the solids, and instead of dancing, we sat as others bounded around us. We were instructed to wave our arms in rhythm above our heads and clap at the end.

When, after a couple weeks, a parent of one of the solids complained, Pippi announced that the solids and their parents did not have to worry because she was planning a Christmas show which would include all of the kids.

When the day of the performance arrived, parents gathered in the auditorium. Many, including my own, had never seen their children in a dance recital. The hall was full.

The time at which the show was to begin came and passed.

Half an hour late, Pippi appeared on stage. She was dressed in her black leotard, striped stockings, and apron.

Clearing her throat, she squinted into the crowd.

"Excuse me," she began.

The crowd quieted.

"Now, I know I invited you here to see the kids in 5C dance, but because we got started late, I'm going to have to cut a couple of the dances. Whoever is left out today will be included in a future dance. Thank you."

Pippi attempted a smile and then glided off stage.

As the lights dimmed, Pippi called out the names of those who would dance. The others would sit on the stage.

Doris and I took our places on the stage. But instead of

sitting quietly, some of the solids, including me, began to cry, which became infectious, and our parents (many of whom were themselves solids) yelled curses at Pippi from the darkened room.

My mother had brought a couple of her friends from the Chelsea Hotel, and they added their own insults. My father meanwhile was using the chaos as an opportunity to sneak out the door in search of an espresso. "Michael!" my mother screamed as she tried to console some of the sobbing children. During this attack, the chosen kids danced.

Pippi's moment as a choreographer of avant-garde elementary school recitals did not last more than a few days. For reasons unknown, Pippi was gone from the school for the next few months. When she finally returned, she leapt from office to office, classroom to classroom, attempting to explain herself. But she stumbled badly on the unhappiness she had sewn, and no one was willing to help her up.

A modern dance.

EYES

MY MOTHER WAS waiting for me when I returned from school. She watched from the doorway as I put my backpack down in the entrance and started to root around the kitchen for a snack.

"Do you know why Ms. Markowitz called and asked to schedule a meeting at school?"

Though Ms. Markowitz had said nothing to me, I knew what this was about.

Following the example of other teachers at the school, Ms. Markowitz was undoubtedly preparing to give out an award to the best student in her class. A lot would go into the decision—class participation, attendance, tests, and helping those who struggled with their homework.

I would never have admitted this to anyone, including my parents, but there really wasn't any question as to who would get the award.

I imagined that at the meeting with my parents, Ms. Markowitz would explain the importance of the award and go over the speech which I would be expected to deliver to the school when I received the honor.

The meeting took place a week later. As soon as Ms. Markowitz entered the room, I began to talk.

"Ms. Markowitz, I've already planned my speech and it will make you very proud. Also, I shall have a few comments on how I think the school could be improved."

"What are you talking about?"

"I shall suggest some additions to the library. Marx Brothers screenplays, for example."

"In an elementary school, Ms. Rips?"

"Why not?! We must raise the bar in public elementary schools, and not allow ourselves to fall behind!" I replied with enthusiasm.

My dad clapped me on the back.

"Ms. Rips," Ms. Markowitz interrupted, "may I remind you that you cannot read."

Heavens!

"Which is why I've asked your parents here today. This school cannot possibly allow you to advance to the next grade unless you can read, and at this point, you are the only one in the class who can't."

Father shifted in his seat. That a school might insist that a student know how to read took him by surprise.

I must confess, though, to being his accomplice. From the few hours I'd devoted to reading, it became clear to me that it was going to be a tough go, and having inherited Father's

dislike for hard work, I was not inclined to put in the effort. In addition, the books my dad read to me were worlds more interesting than what they were giving me at school ("Pat makes a cake. Pat eats the cake."). By the time my childhood quirk blossomed into certifiable illiteracy, I also showed a disturbing disdain for what only I considered "too easy." So there it was: father and daughter, tobogganing off the steep cliff of ignorance.

My mother, who had indulged my father's theories of early childhood education, now felt the need to intervene.

"Be assured, Ms. Markowitz, we shall work with her all summer. Just sign her up for second grade, and if she isn't able to read by the end of the fall, you can send her back."

Ms. Markowitz wouldn't budge.

"Unless she is disabled, your daughter is not leaving second grade."

The truth is that Ms. Markowitz and I got along, and she always had my best interests at heart. To this day, I am fond of her.

"*Myasthenia gravis!*" my father trumpeted.

Silence.

"Muscular weakness of the eye," he translated. "If untreated, there can be damage to the brain, as may be the case here."

His family had been in the optical business in Nebraska for many generations, and the Latin names for ocular oddities was the entirety of his inheritance (and mine).

"Now that you mention it," Ms. Markowitz remarked, "your daughter does not seem to follow the text of the page as carefully as others, which could . . . just possibly . . . be the result of a weakness in the muscles. I've seen it before."

My father nodded—the sort of intelligent nodding that accompanied his most idiotic ideas.

"Yes," Ms. Markowitz concluded, "a muscular problem. Possibly acute. Maybe even brain damage. She has always been the odd man out, not really good at anything. And her hand-eye coordination always seemed off."

With that, I was allowed to pass into second grade.

———

Soon after I was diagnosed by Ms. Markowitz, my parents received the news that the school system set certain conditions for my treatment, which, if not met, would cause the handicapped child (me) to repeat the previous grade . . . meaning back to Ms. Markowitz.

And this is why for an entire year I was forced to spend two hours every day at an experimental eye clinic in midtown Manhattan.

On the first day, my father and I rode the subway to the clinic. It was on the twentieth floor of a hospital complex. The waiting room was filled with unhappy children and their parents, all of them stewing in the chemical odors from the laboratories next door. Unlike me, though, these kids had scary problems—not pretend ones created by their fathers.

After an hour, a man in a lab coat opened the door to the waiting room and called my name. I walked slowly toward him.

I stopped to have a last look at my father as I passed through the door to the laboratories. Given what they were about to do to me, I might never see him again.

But he was not in his seat. Instead, he had made his way to a shelf against the wall, where he was flipping through a stack of medical magazines. I knew exactly what he was up to: he was expanding his vocabulary of rare eye diseases in anticipation of his next cocktail party.

The experiments forced upon me that year depended on who did the testing. Each of the doctors had a different theory about how eye problems were cured, and there was competition between them over whose treatment was most effective. I sat in front of screens as different images and words flashed before my eyes. Liquids were sprayed onto my corneas. Every so often the rotating ophthalmologists would get excited and announce a breakthrough. I personally believe that these experiments ruined my eyesight; I started the year with 20/20 vision and came out needing glasses.

But the eye clinic wasn't the end of it.

Once the doctors had assured my school that my nonexistent physical problem had been cured, I still couldn't read. So from the eye clinic, I was transferred to another program—the GO Project. The GO Project offered free schooling to kids at risk of failing. It was there that I met Nell, a young woman who had been admitted to a graduate program at Harvard and was tutoring until she left for school.

Hearing that I'd spent a year at an experimental eye clinic

caused such a gush of sympathy in Nell that she agreed to spend whatever time was needed to get me to read. Within seven months, I was reading. The first book I ever read on my own was Jerry Seinfeld's *Halloween,* and after that there was no turning back.

My cure did not, however, convince my classmates that I was normal. In addition to thinking I was retarded, they found my false sense of superiority (from my father), the rumor that I was murderous (the pool incident), and my bangs cut at an odd angle (my mother) incredibly distasteful. So there I was: a murderous retard with a bad haircut.

STORMÉ

MY STATUS AT school slowly changed from being a kid who was ignored to one who was bullied.

This was not easy on me, as it was not easy for the others locked in that same cage (the slow, fat, unattractive, and shy), for no matter what you did—how nice you were or how much you pretended that what the other kids said didn't bother you—you would never be released from their taunting. The sound of it was in your head when you went to sleep and there again in the morning.

The effects of this must have shown on my face, because one day, returning home from school, I heard a voice call out to me from across the lobby of the hotel.

"Come over here, baby doll."

I knew the voice. Its owner, Stormé, was a regular in the lobby. She was someone my parents liked, but we'd never spoken.

I had been taught that children should address adults by

"Mr." or "Miss," and since it was unclear which Stormé was, I had decided it was better to avoid Stormé than insult Stormé. That day, for example, Stormé was dressed in military pants, a work shirt, and an opal-and-turquoise necklace.

There was the additional puzzle of Stormé's age. Her face was soft and lineless, but her hair was silver; she had an athletic build, but struggled with the crippled gait of an old person.

Then there was Stormé's race. The skin was whiter than any I'd ever seen, and yet Stormé's hair had the texture of a black person's.

I had met others who were hard to identify by age, sex, or race, but never all three at once. Stormé was a mythological creature.

I crossed the lobby.

"How you doin', baby doll?" The voice was gruff.

As uncomfortable as Stormé made me feel, Stormé struck me as the sort who would be sympathetic to someone who was being bullied.

"The girls in school are making fun of me."

"You tell Stormé why, girlie."

"They think I'm a murderous retard."

"Do you know what Stormé has down there?"

Stormé glanced toward the lower half of her body.

"I'm not sure. I'm still a child."

Stormé tugged on the left leg of her pants.

A pink revolver was strapped to Stormé's ankle.

"That, baby doll, is my best friend. And if anyone gives you trouble, you just give Stormé a call, and my friend and I will come down there and take care of it."

"Thank you, Stormé, but I'm not sure my elementary school allows guns."

"Well then, young lady, Stormé will just shove her boot right up their little asses."

From that day on I went to bed knowing that I had a sexually ambiguous and incredibly violent eighty-year-old woman watching over me. And with that knowledge, who really needs to be afraid of a couple of prepubescent girls?

BUT NOT THE FISH

I LIVED WITHIN a twenty-minute walk of my elementary school, but despite my daily vow to arrive at school early, something always went wrong. And that something was usually my father.

My parents insisted on taking me to school. It was not that they were helicopter parents. They were the opposite. They had nothing else to do. They were like balloons that had escaped a child's grasp—pointlessly floating.

"Focus!" I would plead with my mother as she took a twenty-minute detour from making me breakfast. And my father was forever jumping from one obscurity to another. By the time he and I got to know each other, his life had become a diversion from a task long forgotten.

Each morning began with the intention of getting me to school on time, but my dad would soon get distracted, and the next thing I knew, I was in the middle of the street with him, traffic swerving and honking around us, trying to get a cab to take us the eight blocks between our house and the school. Needless to say, I was never on time.

One day, before I'd finished breakfast, my father, heading out the door, announced that he was picking something up from his tailor (a short Korean gentleman, whose shop was across the street). He would meet me in the lobby of the hotel.

"Don't worry," he said, "we'll have plenty of time to get to school,"

When Father didn't show up in the lobby, I walked across to the tailor. Staring in the window, I noticed the tailor and his wife, tucked behind the counter, going about their business, and there, just in front of the counter, was my father, lying on the floor. Next to him, also on the floor, was a woman. Both of them were surrounded by springing fish.

On the way to school, Father explained what had transpired so that I could better inform my teacher of why I was late:

For years he had been engaged in a "gentle back and forth" with the tailor (which was curious, since I am pretty sure the tailor spoke no English and my father no Korean) about the photographs on the walls of his shop. The photographs, according to Father, were of the tailor flying through the air, striking much larger men, often simultaneously, with his fists, feet, and head.

Father's idea of a "gentle back and forth" was to stare closely at the pictures and then insinuate that they had been doctored, created by the tailor and his wife to discourage

customers from complaining about the prices of their altera-
tions.

The other slice of the "back and forth" was when Father
would spot the Korean leaving to run an errand. He and I
would sneak into the shop and hide in the dressing rooms.
When the Korean returned, we would jump out and try to
scare him or wait until he was with a customer and start making the noises of a child being tortured.

Contrary to father's suggestions, the tailor was a master of
a little-known Korean marshal art—hapkido. In any case, just
before I had arrived at the shop, Father had gone too far and
the tailor had decided to teach him a lesson.

That day, my father learned that the tailor's ability to para-
lyze others had little to do with blows to the head, but with
his knowledge of various points on the human body, which
when pressed in the correct manner sent the strongest men to
the ground.

When handing my father his slacks that morning, the tailor slipped his finger into Father's palm. The pain from the
tailor's finger, combined with whatever my father had been
drinking the night before, caused him to wobble back and
forth and then collapse.

"Knowing that my head was seconds from the floor,"
Father recounted, "I had the presence of mind to flip myself
backwards towards a bag of clothes near the door."

"And the woman?"

"The one on the floor?"

He was avoiding the question.

"Yes, Father, the one on the floor."

He cleared his throat.

"She was carrying the bag."

"So you threw yourself on top of a bag that a woman was holding!"

"Something like that."

"And that knocked her against the fish tank?"

"The details are of no importance. Agility of mind and body, my little friend, saved me."

"But not the fish."

"Sadly no."

"And the woman?"

"The tailor stitched her up."

He paused a moment.

"Do you want me to call your teacher up and talk to her myself?"

"No, that's fine. I'll tell her you have jumping Frenchman's disease."

"That's my girl."

A LEG UP

"HE'S DONE IT again!"

Mr. Crafty was in a state.

"Father?" I replied. It was not really a question.

"Yes, your father. Do you have any idea what he's done?"

"No, but it's probably bad."

"Just ask him!"

Later that evening I did, and this is the story he told:

With Mr. Crafty's paralysis came the slow but noticeable shrinkage of his left leg. For this reason, Mr. Crafty was in frequent need of having his left pant leg lifted.

In the course of his many trips to the tailor, Mr. Crafty, while waiting for his pants, would (like my father) examine the photographs on the wall. After a particularly rough flu season, the tailor, noticing that Mr. Crafty had lost some weight, considerately offered Mr. Crafty a belt that somebody had left in the shop. The tailor assured Mr. Crafty that if he didn't gain the weight back, the tailor would take in the waist.

Mr. Crafty accepted the belt as his first on the road to a black belt, believing it to signal the beginning of his training in hapkido with the tailor as his master.

Father and the fish tank incident had so angered the tailor that he was now refusing to provide services to anyone in the hotel. Mr. Crafty, with his leg shrinking, his pant leg lengthening, and his nonexistent lessons in hapkido suspended, was furious at Father.

This, according to Father's telling, led to a confrontation in the lobby in which Mr. Crafty accused my father of insulting Mr. Crafty's "teacher."

At this point, Uber-Crafty, who had an irrational fondness for my father and had no idea that Mr. Crafty was in imagined training with the Korean, entered the conversation.

As told by my father, the conversations with the Crafties went as follows:

"Your 'teacher'? Who could you possibly be talking about?"

"The man who has been training me in hapkido . . ."

"Trained in *what*? You're barely toilet trained."

"If you would shut your damn mouth, you'd learn of a great teacher. A teacher who was once the student of Choi Yongsool and who, on Shinshu Mountain, received the wisdom of the most skilled and deadly of them all, Takeda Sokaku."

"Nonsense!"

"I now know hand-to-hand and use of all the weapons: jool bong, dan bong, joong bong . . ."

"And your bong, obviously."

"While you waste your morning sleeping, others of us are productive—out each day, first thing, making the country hum."

"Hmm. For the last ten years, half of you has been paralyzed and the other half is the laziest person I know. I don't believe you can even touch your waist, much less your toes. So tell me, who and where is this teacher of yours?"

My father didn't need to be told the answer.

Anyone who had been as beaten and humiliated as my father had been by the tailor would never think to apologize. But not Father. Off he went to beg the tailor to take himself, Mr. Crafty, and all the others in the hotel back.

That, sadly, was not the end of it, for each time that Father returned to the tailor in the following years, he would extract some bit of knowledge regarding pressure points. After a while, Father had assembled enough "lethal wisdom from the East" to believe that he could defend himself against any assault. Among the family of delusions housed in my father's mind, this was the most dangerous.

A CRUSH

ONE OF THE reasons I wanted to get to school early each day was that in the time before class, kids played or talked outside their lockers or met in the cafeteria for breakfast. It was when kids made friends, and that year, I wanted to make friends. I especially wanted to make friends with a particular boy that I had noticed on the playground.

His name was Uhura. He had shiny, dark hair, green eyes, and was very pale and skinny. He was also short. It was the first time in my life that a boy seemed to like me.

On top of this, he was the center of interest, amorous and otherwise, of all the kids.

Oh, yes, about that name.

As reported by my mother, Uhura's mom was a fan of the 1960s television show *Star Trek*, which she watched as a child. She thought, sometimes amusingly, other times seriously, of naming her children, were she to have them, after characters in the show.

When, years later, she was told by her physician that she was having a girl, the soon-to-be mother began to tell her friends and family that her daughter would be named Uhura, giving them plenty of time to arrange for the "Uhura" diaper bags, "Uhura" engraved picture frames, and "Uhura" onesies.

And as everyone, including Uhura's mother, joked about a child named after a *Star Trek* character, they also secretly envied her, thinking that the name would give Uhura that little something extra that every competitive parent in New York wanted for their child.

When Uhura was finally born, it was obvious that she had that little something extra—a penis.

Uhura's penis had been accidentally missed by the sonogram, and then, surprise, there it was. My mom commented, "Bones would not have missed it." Bones, I later learned, was the doctor on the spaceship USS *Enterprise* in *Star Trek*.

As my mother explained it, Uhura's mom, too proud and by now too committed, gave her son the name Uhura, knowing that few would understand its origins and confident that everyone, including herself, would refer to him as "Harry." My mom, recognizing the reference when the two mothers dropped off their kids on the first day of school, developed a friendship with Uhura's mom.

———

One of the odd things about Harry was that whenever my dad walked into the classroom, Harry would throw a toy at him or yell at him or even strike him with his fist. Harry made sure to do this just after his mother left the room and before the teacher arrived. My father was not especially popular with the kids in the class, but Harry was the only one who actually attacked him.

My father would brush this off. He knew, I suspect, of my infatuation.

The attacks lasted until that morning when Harry, his head bent forward, rushed full speed at my father's groin. Relying on his knowledge of human pressure points, Father waited until Harry was just within arm's reach to make his thumb disappear behind Harry's earlobe.

Harry collapsed on the floor, where he lay unconscious, surrounded by a hyperventilating chorus of children and parents.

When Harry was able to talk, he told the teacher that it was my father's fault.

Father, finding the screaming distasteful, had already departed for his morning coffee, and as a result, was not there to defend himself. I tried my best to explain the history of Harry's attacks on my father, but no one was listening. I was hustled to the principal.

The principal's office was a predictably unpleasant place. The only seat for those in trouble was a long wooden bench with no cushions.

After Harry had finished telling his lies about what had happened, the mood turned against me. Sitting on the bench, I began to sweat as the principal and his assistants battered me:

"Where's your father?"

"Was he ever violent with you?" and

"What exactly does he do for a living?"

I inhaled slowly and cracked my knuckles.

"His favorite café; only if you include sarcasm; and if you can figure that out, my mom and I would like to know."

I had a list of real complaints about my father, which I kept in my *I Love Lucy* backpack, but none seemed relevant now.

As to what had actually happened in the classroom that morning, I provided the principal with a concise and calm explanation:

"Uhura started it!"

"Uhura?"

"The chief communications officer on *Star Trek*," I offered.

"Nichelle Nichols attacked your father?"

"No. Harry. He's named after her because they missed his penis."

"He has one now?"

"So I'm told but haven't seen it."

The principal's face told me that he was either new to the story of Harry's genitals or suffered from acid reflux. I pressed on.

"Without thinking, my father did the only thing he knew to do when his groin was threatened—hapkido."

"An ointment?" the principal asked.

Now I was confused. I tried to set things right.

"He picked it up from a Korean."

"Sulu?"

"Was he Korean?" I asked.

The principal felt the story was either too baffling or too close to the loose rock of racial prejudice to pursue, so he let me go. Things quickly returned to normal, except, of course, for Harry's crush on me (which, in retrospect, I suspect I'd invented).

To my list of enemies at the school, which already included the two most popular girls (Greta and Ana—the latter of whom replaced me as Greta's best friend following the pool party), my father added Harry, the cutest boy.

The only two who seemed unaffected by the Harry incident were my father (no surprise there) and mother, who believed (proudly) that her husband had administered to Harry what she referred to as the "Vulcan nerve pinch," and that the entire affair was caused by the hubris of naming a child after a semi-sacred figure.

ARTIE

THE QUIETEST TIME at the hotel was the morning. Unlike those of other residences, crowded with people en route to work, the lobby of the Chelsea was always empty until about noon. The exceptions to this were Stanley (the owner), the one or two people who had passed out in the lobby the night before without ever making it up to their rooms, and the rotation of homeless people who inhabited it.

Stanley's father, who was born in Hungary, purchased the hotel in the 1940s. Stanley took it over when his father became ill. He had been running it ever since.

To Stanley, the hotel residents fell into two groups, those who weren't paying rent and those who weren't paying enough rent, a view that caused great agitation within Stanley. He was there in the lobby every morning to express that agitation.

People in the hotel were not impressed with Stanley's suffering. Stanley, they pointed out, lived in a grand apartment in a very fancy neighborhood far from the hotel. The hotel, in

63

contrast, was well over a hundred years old and showed every year of it.

As tenants passed through the lobby, Stanley would announce how much rent was due and that it had not been paid. It was humiliating. Most of those who owed rent would call the front desk to check if Stanley was in the lobby before exiting the hotel. On those occasions when Stanley left to get a coffee at the Aristocrat, a swarm of tenants would rush out of the hotel.

For those who could not wait for Stanley's caffeine break, there was another option. A couple times a day, an employee from the hotel would move from floor to floor collecting trash on a cart. When full, the cart was taken to the basement on the service elevator, rolled onto a platform, and then lifted up from the basement directly to the sidewalk on Twenty-third Street. Bypassing the lobby, the cart went unnoticed by Stanley. One resident who was behind on their rent would hide among the trash bags. Quite often I would hear, "Hello, Nic," "Give my regards to your parents," or similar greetings from the trash bags as they passed me in the hallway.

But it was not just those who were delinquent on their rents who feared Stanley. Even if a tenant paid on time, Stanley was upset with them, for he took the regular payment of rent as a sign that the tenant was paying too little and that he (Stanley) had been outsmarted in the lease negotiations. My father was in this group.

"How can you live with yourself?" Stanley would ask my father as they passed each other in the lobby.

"Do you have any idea," Stanley continued in a pained tone, "what I pay in electricity? In taxes? And the unions, oh, the unions! They're killing me!"

My father would reply with something like . . .

"Unions? Stanley, the only people who work here are guests you overcharged and who are trying to pay off their bills."

Or . . .

"Stanley, I renegotiated my rent a week ago."

But nothing mattered, for the very next day, putting his arm around Father's shoulders, Stanley continued.

"When you first moved in, I thought, 'This is a good man.' But I must be honest with you: I've been having my doubts. Every day I ask myself, 'Would a good man, with a good family, pay his landlord so little?' It makes me sad to think that."

This would be accompanied by a moistening around Stanley's eyes.

A man who preferred strong coffee in the morning to strong emotion, my father joined the person who hopped on the garbage cart.

But there was one person who didn't care about Stanley.

His name was Artie, and I met him for the first time one morning when I was waiting in the lobby for my mother to take me to school, and Artie came through the front doors. He was in his fifties, with thick dark hair, an athlete's body, a

James Dean swagger, and, as I noticed when he passed, a flask
in his back pocket.

Before Artie reached the elevators, Stanley appeared from
behind the front desk.

"Artie, I need to talk to you."

"You do? Well, that's funny because I need to talk to *you*!"

"Artie," Stanley pleaded, "come into my office and we can
discuss it quietly."

"No! We're going to discuss it *here*!"

Stanley touched Artie's elbow, coaxing him toward the
office. Artie shook it off.

"I know what you want, Stanley."

"You do?"

Artie pulled out his wallet.

"YOU WANT MONEY!"

Stanley waved his hands frantically as if to shake off Artie's
suggestion.

"Artie, please . . ."

Artie was now tapping his wallet against Stanley's chest.

"*How much fucking money do you need, Stanley?* What? You
aren't *rich* enough? What? Living across the street from the
Metropolitan Museum of Fucking Art isn't enough for you?
And you didn't even earn it! You got your money from *Daddy*!
An itty-bitty *daddy's boy*!"

Artie moved in to finish him off, sticking his finger into
Stanley's face.

"*You tell me! Right now!* HOW MUCH FUCKING MATZOH DO YOU NEED?"

"Matzoh? Artie, I beg you . . . ."

"You heard me, Stanley, *mu-cha-cha*."

"Muchacha?"

"Will this do, Mr. G-R-E-E-D-Y?"

Artie pulled something from his wallet and flipped it at Stanley.

"A tensky," announced Artie triumphantly.

Stanley scurried back to his office.

Artie pulled the flask from his back pocket, took a swallow, and by the time it was returned to his pocket, he had, with his other hand, retrieved a bottle of mouthwash from his motorcycle jacket. Standing at the elevator, Artie took a shot, and then, just as the elevator door closed, spat the fluid in an effervescent green arc into the center of a nearby wastebasket.

MY BABYSITTERS

A DOLL IN a dollhouse. That was Jade.

Unlike other babysitters, Jade, who worked in the evenings, was available all day, and with her apartment in the hotel, it was very convenient.

Jade's apartment was decorated with wood paneling, marble floors, leopard skins, and rabbit pelts. Everything was comfortable. Very comfortable. Although her apartment had a balcony and faced the Empire State Building, her shades were always drawn. The apartment was lit with chandeliers, lamps covered in patterned silk shades, and candles. On the shelves was Jade's collection of stuffed quail, raccoons, foxes, and other woodland treasures. Bounding through this was an Egyptian sphinx and miniature greyhound.

My Barbie doll had a small waist; Jade's was smaller. My Barbie had full breasts; Jade's were fuller. Jade's eyes and hair and skin were shinier than Barbie's. So why would I play with dolls when I had Jade?

Unlike Barbie, Jade had a brain. She was smart and witty, and I spent as much time in her apartment as my parents and Jade would allow. Upon my arrival, she would always offer a glass of champagne.

I reminded her every time, "I'm a kid. I don't drink anything but milk, juice, and water."

"Too bad. It's French, from a small vineyard."

Sitting on her red velvet couch, she would bring the glass to her lips, the bubbles never reaching her mouth. Jade did not drink.

It is said her name was not really Jade, but Stacey. That she arrived at the Chelsea Hotel in the middle of the night during a blizzard, a runaway from Florida. It is said she walked from Port Authority to the hotel wearing only a T-shirt, tattered shorts, and flip-flops. That Stanley Bard said she could stay for a few nights, which extended to months, then years. And that in those years she transformed herself from a little girl to a goddess—her home, from a dark, single room without a toilet, to a suite.

It was not to last.

After a year, I noticed that Jade's spotless apartment was coming undone. She was no longer vacuuming every day, and clothing, which was once stored on cushioned hangers, was piling up around the apartment.

"Jade, do you mind if I ask you something?"

"Of course not, dear."

"Well, things are a little messy and you seem . . . worried."

"Is that all?"

"Not exactly . . ."

"Please."

"You have a smell."

Normally, Jade had the most beautiful odor, the result of the perfumes that filled her bathroom shelves. She and I had such fun going through those perfumes: rose, lilac, blueberry, and musk.

"What sort of smell?"

"The smell, well . . ."

"Shalimar?"

I hesitated. "Dog."

Jade sighed. And then explained.

"One day, Nicolaia, you will meet someone and despite how comfortable you are or even happy you are, you won't want to do anything but be with that person."

"When that happens I'll smell like dog?"

Jade continued and told me—and I suspect it was only part of the story—that she had a job which paid her a lot of money, and caused her to work late. She was happy with that job, and it allowed her to buy fancy things and to live in a nice apartment in the hotel.

But one day she met someone. Someone she liked.

"He is studying and doesn't have a lot of money. If I want to be with him, I need to find another job, and the only one I could come up with was betting. I learned from my father when I was a kid, and it's the one way I can make enough to support the two of us."

71

She retreated to a pile of newspapers in the corner, returning with a copy of the *Greyhound Review*, which, according to Jade, was essential to her new life.

For the next hour, she taught me how to handicap "the hounds." Interesting, but not exactly something that was going to help me with elementary school.

What she didn't tell me was that she was moving out of the Chelsea Hotel.

———

With Jade gone, I had no babysitter.

On those evenings when my parents went out, there was a scramble to track down one of the various girls who had looked after me in the past. My parents could never quite remember their names, and if a name was recalled, the number was on a scrap of paper that was lost in a drawer or pocket or inside a book. Often, my parents would give up and haul me along to wherever they were going.

A solution arrived one afternoon when we met a young lady and her mother in the lobby of the Chelsea. They lived in the hotel, and the girl, Dahlia, worked as an au pair. I liked her, and she volunteered her services as a babysitter.

The first few times that Dahlia took care of me, she stayed in our apartment. After playing with me for a while, she would excuse herself, go into my parents' bedroom, and fall asleep. With time, she would take me downstairs to where she and her family lived, so she could sleep in her own bed. If she had other babysitting jobs, she would take me along.

Dahlia's apartment was filled with things her mother had picked up at the flea market and neighborhood antique shops. On the walls were sculptures and paintings by artists in the hotel. Dahlia and her mother had lived there a long time, and the apartment was very crowded.

I should mention that there was always a man lying in a bed just off the living room. That man was Artie, whom I knew from his exchange with Stanley in the lobby. Artie was Dahlia's father.

On the first day I went to their apartment, Artie was in his pajamas, bathrobe, and sunglasses. On his stomach was a camera with a long lens—a scene that was repeated on each of my visits.

At the end of Artie's bed was a television. Completely still, a hunter in his blind, Artie waited until he saw what he was looking for on the screen and then snapped a shot. Every few hours, he would get out of bed, put on his clothes, and leave the apartment. When he came back, he would return to his perch.

Not once, as he passed through the living room, did he acknowledge me or the fact that we had met before.

———

I became close with Dahlia's mother, Colleen. She often returned home with her arms full of flowers, which she would arrange while we talked.

But most exciting was the fact that they, unlike my parents, had animals: a dog, two cats, and a hamster. It was the hamster, Hammie, I liked the most. Once or twice a day I would run downstairs to play with Hammie.

With time, Dahlia began to babysit other kids at the hotel. Two or three years my junior, these kids already had big groups of friends and rarely wanted to spend time with me. I was fine just hanging out with Dahlia's mother instead. There were times, however, when neither Dahlia nor her mom was around, and it would only be Artie and me.

Artie spent each day dormant in bed. Every so often this would be interrupted by a phone call or a visit from someone who wanted to ask him questions. Artie seemed to know about a lot of things.

Artie didn't talk much, and when he did, it wasn't about himself. So it was a long time before I learned that the big canvases on the walls of the hotel, the ones with pictures of FBI agents, men dressed as girls, politicians and actors, were photographs that Artie had taken from the television.

But these were not my favorite of Artie's creations: at the very top of the hotel, suspended from the roof of the tenth floor, were large discs of clear, thin plastic. Infused into those circles were portraits that Artie had taken with his camera. The circles were three or four feet wide, hung from invisible wires, and were lit by multicolored spotlights. When Artie turned on the lights, the photographs would create shadows on the walls—shadows of the people in the portraits. As the discs rotated on their wires, the shadows would mix. Dwight

Eisenhower's face merged into Salvador Dalí's and Muhammad Ali's. For a few minutes, Dwight Dalí Ali was in the hotel.

Though it is true that Artie and I rarely spoke, he understood me. On those rare times when he left the apartment, often wearing a leather jacket and pajamas, he would, as he returned to his bed, toss me a pack of black licorice or a chocolate bar.

THE THEATER

I HAD IMAGINED that by the end of elementary school, my career in musical theater would have been much further along than it was. The problem was clear: Pippi had conspired to give her children the roles (such as the Pea in *The Princess and the Pea* or Thomas in *Thomas the Tank Engine*) that would otherwise have gone to those who, owing to their talent and years of hard work, deserved it—meaning me.

I was complaining to my mother about this when she reminded me of the musicals staged by our local synagogue— the year before, I had played Nancy in *Oliver,* one of their productions. That year, they were doing *Fiddler on the Roof,* Mom's favorite. On Passover, my mother and her family gathered before the television to watch *Fiddler.* During the songs, they would get up to sing and dance around the room, pretending they were leaving the shtetl.

The next day, I walked with Mom to the synagogue. The

director of the musicals, Schmuel, was good enough to meet with us. When Schmuel was not casting, directing, and acting in musicals, he taught Hebrew and made sure there were enough brownies after the bar mitzvahs.

"Of course," he assured me, "you'll be in *Fiddler*. You were my Nancy last year. Besides the main parts—Golde, Tevye, and their three daughters—there are three more daughters, so you will definitely get something."

"Six daughters?" I responded. "I only remember three."

"The others got left out of the movie, but I'm bringing them back."

"And which one would I be?"

"Well there's Tzeitel, Hodel, Chava . . ." Schmuel gazed up at the ceiling and stroked his beard. "And . . . well . . . Prancer, Dancer, and Blixen," he finished quickly. "Maybe you'll be Blixen."

———

With my acting career back on track, I could not have been happier. Returning to the hotel that afternoon, I decided to share my good mood with my friends the Crafties. But they were having a very serious discussion, and when I tried to butt in, I was told to come back in a few minutes. They were, Uber-Crafty explained, trying to work out the details of how to murder someone on the second floor. This was of minor concern to me.

With the Crafties preoccupied, I rolled my good mood across the lobby to the office of Mr. Stanley Bard.

"Mr. Bard. I am sorry to bother you . . ."

"No bother at all. You were born here, grew up here, you are like a daughter to me. A beloved resident of the Chelsea. Your father, on the other hand . . ."

"I have some news," I blurted.

Stanley, who was always on the edge of agitation, began to shake.

"Does it have to do with the Crafties? I heard they're going to murder someone."

"They are," I assured him.

"Me?" he asked.

I shook my head.

"Who, then?"

"The guy with a lot of muscles."

"The one with the platform shoes?" Mr. Bard guessed.

"No, the big bald guy."

Mr. Bard was now stoic.

"No one should murder anyone in this hotel without talk-ing to me first. Remind your friends out there that I'm still the owner of this hotel and someone who cares about all the tenants, even if they are behind on their rent and not one of them is paying what similar hotels, like the Plaza or Carlyle, get for their rooms.

"Did you know the green satin ceiling and green shag

carpet in your apartment was put there by Angie Bowie to complement her pale skin, red hair, and green eyes? What a beauty she was. Between you and me, there was a certain way she looked at me . . ."

"My mom told me ours is the apartment above that one."

"And Marilyn Monroe lived with Arthur Miller just down the hall from you."

"I thought they were on the tenth floor? Anyway, I have some good news."

"They moved around. And now all I have are deadbeats—they complain all the time about the mice. Do you see any mice? I've never seen one. Lies!"

"Mr. Bard, I have good news about my career."

"Did I tell you that Jackie Kennedy used to visit?"

"I don't think so."

"In this office . . . and other places, Jerry's home, but I shouldn't say."

"Mr. Jerry at the front desk?"

"Is there any other? Yes! Jerry Weinstein, my best friend, that conniving S.O.B.—boy, those were the days! Who knows what he has taken from the register?"

Stacks of yellowing papers surrounded him.

"Nicolaia, you said you had something to tell me?"

"Very good news, Mr. Bard. Do you know Blixen?"

"Of course! My grandmother's were the thinnest in the neighborhood."

"Two thin, Jewish grandmothers? Unusual."

"*No*, not my grandmothers. The blintzes! They were the thinnest crêpes in the neighborhood; she used to cook them on the back of the pan, a little cottage cheese and cherry jam . . . "

"Mr. Bard, I am talking about Tevye's daughter Blixen."

"Blixen, the reindeer?! Who's playing Tevye?"

"Maybe Schmuel—he was my husband, Bill Sikes, in *Oliver*. He reminds me of you."

"People have always said I would make a great Tevye. I think Jerry said it. Years ago when we were . . . Wait a minute, where is that good for nothing Jerry?"

He stared off to the side, driving recklessly into his memory.

I stepped quietly out of his office. As I closed the door, I looked back at Mr. Bard—the Tevye of the Chelsea Hotel, an eccentric yet lovable bundle of anxiety.

In the end, the Hebrew School cast a boy named Saul to play Tevye. He had a high voice and long blond hair. I was chosen as Golde, his wife, which meant that for the first time in any production of *Fiddler*, Tevye had less facial hair than the woman he married. Golde was a good role; she had many songs and wasn't killed by pogroms. My cousin Tillie was Blixen.

REBECCA

WHEN OUR TEACHER, Rebecca, young and attractive, walked into our fifth-grade class, there was only one thought in the room: "Fancy." Black dress, pumps, fine stockings—all stylish and expensive in that obviously not-obvious way that refined people have.

Here was someone who appreciated the gravity of the superficial (her haircut and nails alone took a day at the salon). She would have no interest in homework or lectures.

It took only a couple days to realize how wrong we were.

When two boys were caught talking during one of her lectures, she told them to stop or they would have "to sit in the hallway." When they continued, Rebecca, dragging two chairs behind her, led them outside.

The next day the chairs remained in the hallway.

And the next, and the next, until it became apparent that when Rebecca had told them that they would have to sit in the hallway, she meant that they would be spending the rest of the year there.

When their parents complained, pointing out that they were "good boys," Rebecca gestured toward the other classrooms in the hall.

"Surely," Rebecca replied, "such good boys will be welcome in someone else's class. But not here."

End of discussion.

Rebecca's no-talking-in-class rule was the first of many.

After I received a failing grade on an art project (a portrait of my grandmother), my baffled mother studied the difference between it and my earlier "A" drawings. With some inspection it became clear to my mother that Rebecca wanted all drawings to have their backgrounds completely filled in. Having detected a speck or two of white from the paper below the drawing of my grandmother, Rebecca scrawled a red "F" across Grandma's face.

"There is no right way to express yourself," my mother comforted me. "But you also need to learn to give teachers what they want—especially Rebecca."

Compared to the punishing way that kids often treated each other, Rebecca's insistence that we fill in the white spaces behind Grandma's head seemed a light sentence.

As kids were expelled and others, weakening under the weight of Rebecca's rules, switched teachers or schools, the number of kids in her class shrank. None of this seemed to bother Rebecca.

For those of us who held out, though miserable, we sensed that we were learning in a way that we never had before. And that was because Rebecca didn't care if we liked her. For her, there was only one thought: getting the most important ideas of literature, science, and current events into our undeveloped brains as deeply and quickly as possible.

Every day, she was there in the classroom, waiting solemnly, dressed head-to-toe in black, ready to cut out bad ideas and replace them with healthy material, a fashionable surgeon.

In addition to the assignments required by the school, Rebecca insisted that each of us complete a long writing project. We could do almost anything, but it had to focus on a single subject.

As we wrote, she would offer comments, making sure that by the time the project was complete, it was as close to perfect as our little minds could get it. As a gift, she had all of our writings printed and bound, with an engraved cover.

Rebecca was not the most popular teacher in the school. Other teachers, burdened by the kids they had to take in from Rebecca's class, disliked Rebecca; administrators, sensing her disapproval, avoided her. And Rebecca, aware of this, ignored everyone.

If there was one person who was as friendless as I was at school, it was Rebecca.

Fifth grade brought new responsibilities, one of which was the privilege of spending lunch outside the school grounds. This seemingly innocuous activity was the most exciting part of the day, a foray into the real world. We had forty-five minutes to pick up food from a nearby deli and return to class. The only limitations were that we could not go beyond a three-block radius and we couldn't go out without someone else—a "buddy."

On the first day, I wandered over to two girls who were getting ready to leave for lunch.

"Excuse me, would it be okay if I came out with you guys? I don't have a buddy."

The first girl turned to her friend and frowned. "What did *it* say?"

The other girl shrugged.

"*It* can't come with us."

With that, they walked away.

This might explain why when Rebecca asked if there was anyone who wanted to spend their lunch hour helping her clean the classroom (unsurprisingly, she was also fixated upon keeping an immaculate work space), I alone raised my hand. Not that I had a better option. Lunchtime meant sitting alone in the cafeteria or taking my lunch to some corner of the school where I wouldn't be seen.

Cleaning up Rebecca's classroom turned into a regular job. I would spend fifteen to twenty minutes putting things away and sweeping, and then sit down at a desk and eat my lunch. Not a word was exchanged with Rebecca. But she seemed to tolerate having me there, and I liked the idea of having a place to go.

Not once during that year did anyone else join Rebecca for

lunch, nor did she ever leave the classroom. Rebecca seemed unbothered by the fact that the only one in the school who wanted to hang out with her was me.

One day, Rebecca informed me that she would not be in class the next couple days. I worried that she had been fired.

A day or two later, I met my mother in a coffee shop after school. She slid a picture across the table. It was a photograph of President Obama in the White House. He was in deep conversation with someone with whom he was obviously friendly. Rebecca.

WINTER VALLEY

ONCE A YEAR my elementary school treated its fifth-grade students to two or three days in the countryside. Kids could hike or swim in a lake or just wander around. In the evening, everyone gathered wood and built fires. The place we went was Winter Valley. Everyone looked forward to it, especially me.

Unpopular kids tell themselves that if they have a chance to get out of school and be with kids in a different setting, it will be easier to make friends. Winter Valley was perfect for this: there were plenty of group activities, and the kids slept together in log cabins.

My class trip to Winter Valley was scheduled for February. Though I didn't much like the cold, I was thrilled. It was all I could think about. I read about the trees and animals that I would see, how to build a fire and make friendship bracelets. I had been collecting magazines on "country living" for years, hoping that one day my parents would move us to a woodsy place.

I had asked my parents to come on the trip as the chaperones, but that was never going to happen. My father, though still young, gave the convincing appearance of having been around for a couple of centuries, and on the rare occasion that he left his armchair, could be found at the nearest café. My mother had also refused. Her idea of traveling was to places like Tashkent or Bamako, not Winter Valley with a group of kids.

My mom packed me a bag full of my favorite clothing, all of which could have doubled as maternity wear. As I boarded the bus, full of expectation and clothed in T.J.Maxx's finest, my parents waved good-bye to me from the street.

On the bus sat my classmates, a couple teachers from the school, and Doris's mom, our chaperone.

As soon as we left the parking lot, the kids started singing "I Kissed a Girl" by Katy Perry. As I joined them, something came out of my mouth along with the notes and words.

As an infant, I had suffered from motion sickness. For this reason, when Mom and I traveled, she would make a point of avoiding buses, boats, and long car rides. So careful was she that I'd forgotten that I even had the problem.

What this meant was that in addition to my voice that morning I was able to contribute to the song the masticated contents of my last meal. I spent the rest of the trip with my head in a plastic bag.

———

As soon as we arrived at Winter Valley, I raced off in search of a bathroom.

When I returned to the bus, my classmates were gone. I waited, but the gentlemen who I had assumed had been assigned to carry my bags to the cabin did not appear. Full of the camping spirit, I took hold of my new pink Hannah Montana bag and, with the assistance of a previously unknown strength, rolled it up the hill to Chief True Eagle Cabin, my assigned residence.

Inside, I was greeted by Doris's mom. She walked me to the one unoccupied bed at the very back of the room. It was the only single bed in a room full of bunks.

Where, I wondered, were the reading chairs, duvets, and hand-painted wallpapers that I'd seen in the country living magazines?

There were only gray walls, metal bunk beds, and a muddied beige carpet. Doris's mom sensed my disappointment.

"For your information," she lectured, "Chief True Eagle was not interested in trivial things."

"Could you find me a chief who was?"

"Here is your bed," replied Doris's mom, and then she turned to leave.

I interrupted her departure.

"Excuse me. Do you smell something?"

Doris's mom sniffed. An expression of disgust flooded her face.

After the deafening sound of a certain bathroom appliance, one of my classmates emerged from a door not two feet from my bed. I realized then why my bed had remained unoccupied.

Did I mention that it was snowing? It was the type of snowfall dense enough to make snowmen or throw snowballs. This snow overwhelmed the cabins, trees, and everything beyond until nothing was visible.

Snow like this hadn't been seen at Winter Valley for over a decade. So amazing was it that the staff of the camp, after a dinnertime discussion with the parents and teachers, decided that the next day we would all go snowshoeing on a nearby mountain. Everyone was excited.

———

At exactly eight o'clock the next morning, we gathered at the edge of the camp. The sky was clear.

Together, we moved toward the mountain, and as we climbed, the counselors gave us a history of the area. Trees and animals and birds were discussed. I felt connected to our group, marching in the same direction, toward the same adventure.

After an hour or two of walking, we reached the point at which we could go no farther. The snow was too deep.

The people I knew in New York were not exactly the snow-shoeing sort and I was at a loss as to what to do. On top of this, I was clumsy.

I drifted behind.

When the distance between me and the group was so great that I could no longer see them, I became nervous. Before I could call out, I began to fall forward.

My head screwed into the snow. The cold shocked me. After a minute or two, a horned animal, possibly a unicorn, galloped toward me. I was in a tapestry—ladies and knights floating in the distance as the beast made its way to my side.

Suddenly I was being hoisted from the snow, the steamy breath of the unicorn warming my face. My eyes began to clear.

It was Doris's mom.

Witnessing my fall, she had come snowshoeing down the hill. Not all that good in snowshoes herself, she jerked back and forth, waving her poles in the air above her head.

But I was not in a position to say anything unkind about Doris's mom. She was more fretful about her child than most of the parents at school, but she was one of the few willing to come with us to Winter Valley and the only parent willing to face the mountain beside us.

Having lifted me out of the snow, Doris's mom turned to lead us back up the hill, but upon taking her first step, she lurched up and over her own snowshoes. As soon as she hit the snow, she began to somersault. There was no one below to stop her tumbling, so I watched as she, a groaning, growing orb of whiteness, disappeared down the hill.

Where she ended up, I do not know. But it took an hour for the instructors to find her.

By the time I returned to the camp, everyone was convinced that I was responsible for whatever had happened to Doris's mom. There was even a rumor that I'd pushed her. For the remaining days at Winter Valley, no one spoke to me; I was not included in group activities; and at the meals, I sat alone.

Just before we returned to New York, word came back to us that Doris's mom was alive and conscious but had broken a number of bones and would be in the hospital for a couple weeks. I could not have felt worse about this.

Despite my efforts to move forward, to find friends, to be appreciated in some way, I was back at that pool party, the baby throwing me off balance, the look on the faces of the others. My life was folding back on itself.

―――

In school the following Monday, it was clear that my place was fixed: I would, for the rest of my life, be known as the least popular kid in the elementary school. Before Winter Valley, I had comforted myself with the thought that there was time for things to change. Now it was too close to graduation. Doris's mom was still in the hospital, and she was not getting out any time soon. In fact, the doctors were now saying that she would need another operation.

One morning, my mother sent me to school with a nicely wrapped package for Doris's mother. When I handed it to Doris, I assured her that her mom was going to love the gift, though I had not bothered to ask my mother what was inside.

Because I'd delivered the gift on the very day that Doris's mom was scheduled for her second operation, Doris was able to unwrap it for her as soon as she awoke. So after a day of having titanium rods inserted into her arm, Doris's mom opened her eyes to a wicker basket filled with hand creams, each with a cheery message from my mother.

"Having trouble with your cuticles? Try this."

When my father, never wanting to upset my mother, had told her the Winter Valley story, he poured a little too much fabric softener into it, so that she had entirely the wrong idea about what had happened to Doris's mom.

The unexpected, but welcome, effect of this was that I was given a brief rest from people disliking me, as teachers, parents, and even some students came to believe that my unfortunate personality was less my doing than the weedy outgrowth of a deranged couple.

THE TRAITOR

THE HOTEL WAS close enough to my elementary school that I could walk home. Most of the other kids lived farther away and took the public bus. Every day, Mother would meet me at the school, and often we would stop for tea on our way home.

As a result of the bonding I had witnessed on the bus ride to Winter Valley (a bonding I was excluded from by nausea), I became convinced that if I commuted with my classmates, they would eventually come to accept me. At the very least, I would get an idea of what they liked to talk about, and that would help me socialize. After lengthy negotiations, my parents agreed to buy me a Metrocard for the NYC bus. My mother worried about this because she thought the bus was dangerous, even though many of my classmates took it as well.

For the first few trips, everything went as I hoped. Though no one spoke to me, I was able to overhear what the other kids were saying, and in a notebook, I would write down the names of the singers, television shows, and computer games they mentioned.

It was not very long into this new routine that I noticed some girls gathering at the back of the bus, laughing. I didn't pay much attention until one day when the bus was very crowded, and I ended up in one of the back seats. It was then that I saw why they were laughing.

A woman in torn blue-and-yellow checkered overalls, no helmet, with paint splattered across her hands and face was cycling madly, dangerously, in back of the bus.

My mom.

Still very concerned about me, she had decided that if she couldn't walk me home, she would secretly follow me, pedaling after the bus until I reached the hotel. Her outfit was what she wore when she was in her art studio.

Once Mom gave up modeling, she was happy to never worry again about what she looked like when she appeared in public; so it was not unusual for her to go around in her shredded overalls, paint on her face, hair a mess.

Even this, to my amazement and envy, did not affect her beauty. But it made for an odd sight, and I stopped taking the bus.

For the few days I was on the bus, my classmates talked mostly about middle school—a concern we all shared because our elementary school ended after fifth grade.

We were required to list five different public schools (in any borough) in order of preference. Some of the schools asked for interviews and supplementary material. Our choices were then fed into a citywide computer program where schools would process our answers. If a student didn't get into their first choice, the computer would shuffle down their list of schools until there was a match.

Parents, school counselors, and teachers were obsessed with the selection process. Parents would spend months looking at schools, reading through pages of catalogues and "inside" guides, and forcing their children to endure endless interviews. Worst of all, we would have to go through it again when we applied to high school. This was how the New York public school system worked, and it was brutal.

If we did not get accepted into the handful of superior middle schools, we would not, when it came time to apply to high school, matriculate into the two or three superior high schools—which meant that we were doomed for college, and thus for life. It was that competitive. Or so everyone thought.

While we skidded down the middle school abyss, a small number of parents received an e-mail from our teacher, Rebecca.

She explained to these parents that their son or daughter was very smart, brilliant even, and that she (Rebecca) wanted to make certain their child got into a top middle school. Having worked in the school system for many years, Rebecca knew teachers and admissions officers at middle schools across the city and was therefore in a position, she assured the parents, to be very useful.

There were two conditions: the parents whom Rebecca contacted were not allowed to tell anyone that Rebecca was helping them, and they were never to speak to Rebecca about this other than through e-mails.

The parents, of course, agreed.

With that, Rebecca began a lengthy e-mail exchange with these lucky parents in which she described the schools she felt were right for their kids and then set out a strategy for getting them in. Rebecca explained to them that there were a handful of middle schools, all outside the borough of Manhattan, which were little known to the public but full of exceptional teachers.

More important, each of these middle schools boasted exceptional records of getting their students into the best high schools. At these places Rebecca knew someone who could make certain that the child was admitted.

In exchange for Rebecca's help, the parents became slaves to Rebecca: she would send them e-mails demanding that they make cupcakes and drop them off by the end of the day or leave their offices to return a library book that their kid had borrowed from the school.

When I finally heard about this through the grapevine of elementary school gossips, I was very, very upset. My parents were not included in Rebecca's little group, which meant that she didn't care about me.

I already knew that I was not an especially pretty girl (I related more to the "before" people in self-help ads than the "afters") and that I wasn't all that likable and that some of my interests (Groucho Marx and Oscar Wilde) were different from those of other students. But I knew that when I worked hard, I could usually do as well as the others in my class.

But apparently not, for Rebecca—with whom I had come to identify and whom I considered a friend—had clearly ditched me. I'd been betrayed and didn't know what to do about it.

The sadness inside me was not budging, no matter how hard I pushed at it or how many times I cried.

With Rebecca having abandoned me, the whole thing with Doris's mom, and no one at the school ever wanting to be anywhere near me, I was friendless. I didn't care about playdates or birthday parties or sleepovers—those were out of the question; I just wanted someone to talk to me—a "How are you?" "Pleasant day, isn't it?" would have been nice. But it wasn't going to happen.

I needed a plan.

Once or twice a year, Luca (our neighbor at the hotel) would throw a costume party. There were always thirty or forty people dressed as kings, queens, gangsters and starlets, long-dead painters, poets, and cartoon characters.

Girls in my school liked to get dressed up, so why not plan a princess party? I asked my mom about it, and she thought it was a great idea.

We came up with the idea of the Princess Banquet.

Half a dozen girls received handwritten invitations to meet me at the Chelsea Hotel on a certain date and time.

On the night of the party, I stood outside the hotel in my Belle costume, waiting for the princesses to arrive. The girls showed up on time, all in costume, and I escorted them through the lobby.

I pointed out the sculpture of the obese pink woman swinging above our heads, her plump legs dangling.

The princesses stared.

Beneath the Pink Lady were the Crafties. They were, as usual, arguing. I called out to them.

"These are the princesses I was telling you about!"

Mr. Crafty stood up.

"I hope you princesses have a fucking good time."

It was one of the nicest things I'd ever heard him say.

I led the girls to the elevator. As the door opened and a crowd rushed out, I explained to the princesses that Stanley, the manager, must be out for dinner. The girls shuffled inside.

The elevator doors opened on the second floor.

A woman in a motorized wheelchair entered. Dressed in black, hunched over, her stringy black and white hair covered all but her toothless scowl. She pushed herself into the pack of princesses.

"BACK, MIDGETS!"

I turned to the girls and made my most polite introduction.

"Smiley, Princesses. Princesses, Smiley. My mom says Smiley is one of the best artists ever."

As the door closed, Smiley spun her chair, pinning Rapunzel against the wall.

"Where'd you take my electricity?"

"I don't know," cried Rapunzel. "I want to go home."

"Me too," added Cinderella.

"You all have nice homes," barked Smiley. "No one sneaks in at night and steals your heat. You don't have to sleep in a lawn chair at the front door to catch them."

Mulan looked mystified. "Who's stealing your heat?"

Smiley's mouth twisted. "They don't leave calling cards."

The people in the hotel understood that Smiley would accuse each of them, over the years, of stealing her paintings, along with her electricity, her jewelry, and her thoughts. Despite this, the people in the Chelsea liked her and she liked them.

The elevator doors opened onto the sixth floor, and the princesses ran out.

My mom and I had set a long table for dinner. There was an ironed lace tablecloth, which had been my grandmother's, flowers, candles, music, and four courses, with plenty of cakes and pies, served by a waiter from El Quijote, the Spanish restaurant in the lobby. I had been inspired by the ball scene in *Cinderella*.

The girls calmed down, and everything seemed back on track.

My chair was at the head of the table, where Mom placed a pillow to give the effect of a throne. When the princesses took their seats, I knew the banquet was a success. The princesses would go to school the next day and tell their friends, and they would tell their friends. Girls would beg me for an invitation.

Halfway through the dinner, there was a knock at the door. Mother opened it.

"I apologize for the interruption, but is your husband at home? I could use a word or two."

El Capitan.

But wasn't the Capitan's visit that evening the most brilliant luck? Who better to drop in on the Princess Banquet than a man in uniform with a foreign accent.

"He's visiting his mom in Omaha, but when he returns, I'll tell him to find you."

The door began to close. But I was determined not to let the Capitan get away.

"Capitan, there are some princesses I would like you to meet."

"I am certain that the Capitan has many things to do. And now is not a good time for him," Mom insisted.

"Princesses?" the Capitan responded from the door. "I have known a few in my day, so it would not surprise me if I've already had the pleasure of meeting one or two of your guests."

"But Capitan . . ." my mother began.

The Capitan entered the Princess Banquet.

A gasp from the princesses.

The Capitan was not in his uniform. The Capitan was not in anything—save his briefs.

His black hair, usually combed tight against his scalp, was off in various directions; his monocle was cracked and dangling around his neck; and his right arm was red and swelling.

"Good evening, Your Highnesses."

Rapunzel wheezed, "Please. I want to go home!"

"And I would like to go home as well, my dear princess, but it has been desecrated. The Lady Hammersmith, my beloved, has not been right in the head, which is why I need to visit with the man of the house, my advisor. A magnificent example of pomposity!"

"Lady Hammersmith or my father?" I asked, though I probably knew the answer.

"Why, your father: an ass of the most excellent sort."

Mother, who was now setting a place for the Capitan, glanced at his arm.

"The hospital?"

"No. I am not seriously injured, though I might well have been. While Lady Hammersmith's intentions were not clear, her first blow with the ax brought down the canopy of my bed, bruising my head and raising me from my sleep. But for this, I am not certain what would have happened."

"An ax?" I asked.

"A francisca to be exact—acquired from an antiquarian in the south of France," he reflected.

"And the bed?" my mother called, now back in the kitchen.

Mother had always admired that bed. Set in the middle of the Capitan's apartment, it was over two hundred years old and, according to the Capitan, made of the finest wood in the Far East.

"Kindling."

With that, Mother began slicing the cakes and pies for the princesses, though none of them seemed hungry.

Minutes before, I'd imagined future dinners with my many new friends, also with flowers, cakes, pies, and ice cream. But that picture was toppling, shaken by what I knew the princesses would be saying the next day about me and the place where I lived.

As the princesses left the apartment, the Capitan bowed to each, his mood improved by the cake.

My mood, however, could not have been improved.

I didn't understand the girls' reaction to my home. I'd lived at the Chelsea all my life. The bickering Crafties amused me. I was worried for Smiley, not scared. And as to the Capitan, he and Lady Hammersmith would make up over lobster and cocktails at El Quijote, as they always did.

I discovered a new emotion that evening—embarrassment.

I was embarrassed by Stormé and Smiley and the Crafties and everyone else who had been kind to me. The Chelsea Hotel was no longer a shining castle, it was a crumbling outpost of outcasts, outbursts, and failure. Those I loved weren't captains, knights, and ladies, they were addicts and cripples and prostitutes. From that day on I dreaded becoming like them. I strived to distance myself and to fit in elsewhere.

That day I learned I had to keep my Chelsea Hotel to myself. I was ashamed.

MY FRIEND FAN

"YOUR MOOD HAS changed, and I'm worried," my mother greeted me as I came through the door.

"Nonsense. Couldn't be cheerier."

"You can't fool me. You're in a bad state."

"It could be the gout."

"Little girls don't have gout."

"Dad had gout when he was a teenager."

"He is a man of singular achievements. What you need is someone you can talk to about your problems."

To be honest, I was still upset over the business with the princesses. And while I would normally share my troubles with the Crafties, I didn't really want to see them. I avoided the lobby as much as possible.

"I'll find someone at school," I said weakly.

My mother became determined to find me a friend. If you had asked my parents why I didn't have any, they would have said that because I had difficulty learning to read and write,

I was treated as a "special" kid, spending most of my school time in individual instruction and not with my class. Given my reputation for being retarded, she knew it was going to take them awhile to find a friend for me.

In the meantime, my parents bought me a few steps down from human interaction: a hamster. They knew I loved Hammie (Artie's hamster) and thought I'd enjoy one of my own.

The hamster I picked was white and fluffy and I named her Cream Puff. Appropriate to her appearance, she had a sweet personality. I kept her cage in my room and each day would feed her, change her water, and take her for walks.

Taking her for "walks" was complicated. Cream Puff, being no more than a couple inches long, could easily disappear into crevices of the hotel and there encounter all sorts of dangerous things.

The answer to this problem was the hamster ball. Unscrewing the top, I inserted Cream Puff into the translucent sphere and then screwed the top back on the ball. Placing it on the floor, Cream Puff would run in one direction or another, the ball rolling with her, protecting her from other animals and making certain that she did not crawl out a door or window or into the walls.

I would take Cream Puff into the hallway and let her run around. Since the hallways in the Chelsea are long and wide, it proved great fun for Cream Puff. I imagined that from inside the ball, the world whirled by in spinning flashes of light and color—like rolling inside a kaleidoscope. Cream Puff became my happiness, and I could be found sitting in the hallway for hours watching her roll around and around.

To add to the riches, halfway through the year, my parents found a girl who would be my friend—Fan O'Malley.

Fan was clever and sunny and, more important from my parents' point of view, she showed unusual concern for other kids, always asking questions about what was going on in their lives and being helpful to them when needed. Unlike the other kids in the school, Fan was not all knotted up about where she was going to middle school. The reason for this, it seemed to me, was pretty straightforward: if you were born in rural China, lived in a Chinese orphanage, and then forced to adapt to life in New York City, middle schools don't seem all that important.

Fan and I started hanging out together, and to my surprise, everything I had perceived about her was true: Fan was kind to others and was always there to listen and give good advice. On top of this, she had her own paper shredder. Shredding paper in Fan's bedroom became a favorite pastime of mine.

One day while Fan watched as I shredded paper, I asked her if she wanted to join me. She said no. She just felt happy that others were enjoying themselves, knowing that the shredder was there in case she ever needed it.

That's the kind of kid Fan was.

THE TRAITOR REVEALED

AS I MENTIONED, Rebecca was a stickler for the rules. Anyone who was late to class, as I was that day, risked being thrown out. I was late because my dad had decided to jump behind the counter and show the neighborhood barista how to make a proper espresso.

Hurrying up the six flights of stairs to my classroom and mulling over the excuses I might offer, I decided to play it cool. Say nothing, I thought, and take your seat. Appear detached and bored. No need to apologize. Today, I was going to stand up to her.

"It is not my fault I'm late!" I shouted out as soon as I entered the classroom.

But when I glanced at Rebecca, I was surprised at what I saw: the always taut and tidy Rebecca held her face in her hands.

I felt a bold tap on my shoulder; turning around, I came face to face with Beatrice Bendel, a Sri Lankan girl.

She plopped in the chair next to me and started to whisper.

I tried to brush her off, but Beatrice refused. And it was a good thing, for when I finally paid attention, I heard this:

". . . and then created a *Gmail*. And you know what else, the *police* think that it's the parent of someone in our class! I think it's David's dad; he always hated Rebecca—especially when she called David a dope. What do you think?!"

I told her that I'd need a few more details.

Beatrice came through:

Just after we'd all submitted our applications for middle school, Jessie's mom, one of the parents who had been included in Rebecca's secret circle, took Rebecca aside to thank her for her help. According to my father, their conversation went something like this:

"Rebecca, I just wanted to tell you how much I appreciate what you did for us."

"You're welcome, but it's what I try to do for all the kids . . ."

"Rebecca, I am sure about that, but we would never have thought of sending our daughter to middle school in Staten Island without you."

"Staten Island?"

Jessie's mother had been around the block, and what she saw on Rebecca's face was the look of a person who had just experienced something utterly repulsive. As if Jessie's mom had dumped red wine all over Rebecca's Chanel suit.

But as horrible as this was for Rebecca, it was worse for

Jessie's mom, since it was now obvious to her that the person with whom she had been communicating about her daughter's applications to middle school was not Rebecca. And if not, then who?

Another teacher? A parent? Someone who hated her child?

———

The principal spent days attempting to find Fake Rebecca. But no luck.

The principal appealed to Fake Rebecca to come forward through an announcement on the loudspeakers, but that didn't work either.

He called the police.

The police seized computers and interrogated teachers, parents, and administrators. The police had profilers analyze Fake Rebecca.

A couple weeks later, the police issued their report. What they discovered was that Fake Rebecca was not in touch with just a handful of parents, but with every parent in the class, proposing to each that they should send their children to generally obscure middle schools, often not in the borough of Manhattan and few being a school that anyone (especially Rebecca) would recommend.

The police also reported that Fake Rebecca was most likely the parent of a student or former student of Rebecca's— someone who was irritated at how Rebecca had treated their child. Though it was a good theory, it didn't narrow the suspects, given the number of parents whom Rebecca had irritated over the years.

The e-mails from Fake Rebecca were so convincingly in the words and tone of Rebecca that it had to be an adult. Also, Fake Rebecca was having daily e-mail exchanges with large numbers of people; only an adult with time during the day could have pulled it off. Someone who was self-employed, a writer or freelance editor, for example.

It occurred to me that it might be you-know-who. But I dismissed the thought: Fake Rebecca required too much energy for my father to sustain over anything more than a couple hours on a nice afternoon with a gin and tonic.

However, the worst news for any parents that had actually taken Fake Rebecca's direction had yet to arrive. It was too late to change the selections.

While the parents were dealing with this shock, Sherry Wisenhower, a well-liked girl in my class, came forward to report that someone had created a fake e-mail address for her and was sending insulting messages to kids in the class. Those kids, assuming the e-mails were from Sherry, had turned on her.

Sherry's mom noticed what she believed to be similarities in the language used by the Sherry Impersonator and Fake Rebecca. From this, she concluded that they were one and the same.

This led Sherry's mom (Mrs. Wisenhower) to write this letter:

Dear Rebecca,

I believe Fan is the one who was pretending to be you. The reason I think it's Fan is because Fan is a mean girl. She pretends like she's not, but she is.

Yours sincerely,

Mrs. Amy Wisenhower

For the Wisenhowers, Fan, who had started out as an itch in the third grade, had become a full-blown rash by fifth, with the Wisenhowers doing whatever they could to promote their daughter at Fan's expense.

A day or two later, Amy received Rebecca's response:

Dear Ms. Wisenhower,

Though I appreciate your efforts to find the person who has been impersonating me, it troubles me that you should think it is Fan, who, as everyone knows, is extremely smart and seems to always have the best interests of her classmates in mind.

If you should have any other ideas, please let me know. We are all concerned about getting to the bottom of this.

Sincerely,

Rebecca

P.S. Please tell me why you think Fan is a "mean girl." That is not a very nice thing to say about someone.

The response was immediate.

Dear Rebecca,

Why is Fan a mean girl?! Well, when Sherry tells other kids about her grades (which you know are always very high), Fan gets angry and says that she has higher grades than Sherry and that Sherry's parents have the money to pay for tutors. That is why I told Sherry to stop having anything to do with Fan.

Yours,

Mrs. Amy Wisenhower

If anyone was ever curious about the intelligence of the Wisenhowers, they would not need to search much beyond Mrs. Wisenhower, who was actually sending the above e-mails to the Fake Rebecca. Mrs. Wisenhower caught wind of this only when the last e-mail bounced back. The e-mail account of the Fake Rebecca had been shut down.

I could hear the sound of the paper shredder.

———

The police detective who interviewed Fan told the principal that he'd "interrogated Mafia capos who were harder to break." But Fan eventually confessed. And with that confession came the explanation for what she'd done.

Fan, who, unknown to anyone, wanted to attend a particular and very selective middle school, determined that, given the nature of the computer program that the city used in selecting middle schools, it would be to her advantage if the other students in our class listed middle schools outside of Manhattan as their first choice.

The rest was easy: pick the teacher whom parents were most likely to trust on the question of middle schools (Rebecca); let these parents believe that they were the only ones whom Rebecca chose to assist; and then complete the deception by including in the e-mails the sort of demands that were typical of Rebecca—bring cupcakes to the school, return library books, spring off the toilet when necessary.

When Fan was finally exposed, the reaction against her was so extreme (certain parents threatened to kill her) that Fan and her parents were placed in what was essentially an elementary school protection program. Their addresses, e-mails, and telephone numbers were changed, and Fan was relocated to a school in Chinatown, where the Caucasian parents would have trouble finding her.

If I am being entirely honest here I must confess to having half-suspected that it was Fan all along, but what was I going to do? Snitch on one of my few real friends?

Rebecca, disgusted with the whole affair and insulted that people would mistake her for anyone as devious as Fake Rebecca, left the school and quit teaching altogether.

You may be wondering what happened to me. The answer is that when Fan went to contact my mother via e-mail, Fan misspelled her name.

After Fan's e-mail to my mother bounced back, Fan tried my father's e-mail. That went through, but it made no difference, since he hadn't checked his e-mail in years. So Fan was never able to reach my parents, and I put in my choices unaffected by Fake Rebecca.

As it turned out, amidst all of this drama, I got into the middle school that was first on my list. I could only assume that my success came because it was also the middle school of Fan's dreams and she managed to divert the more deserving applicants.

In the end, Fan proved to be a very good friend.

MIDDLE
SCHOOL

THE SEWER AND THE CUTTER

A GIRL (SPOILER: me) walks into an auditorium on the first day of middle school. She finds there a large gathering of kids, parents, and teachers, and in front of them all, the principal, who will begin to tell everyone how very excited he is about the school year, how hard he and his staff worked over the summer to get things ready for the first day of class, and how he knows that everyone is going to have a great year.

This girl, tall and chubby for her age, her frizzy brown hair pulled back into a ponytail, sighs happily. She is optimistic. New friends. New crushes. A fresh start.

———

Standing next to me was a girl who, clearly upset about the new school, had begun to cry.

"Look," I whispered idiotically, "it could be worse."

She stared back, anxious, wanting to be convinced. I needed to say something. I settled on a story I had been told that very morning by Jerry, the manager of the front desk at the Chelsea.

"There were two old Jewish men who worked together in a clothing factory," I began. "It was crowded and hot, and they stood on their feet all day long."

Ignoring her bewildered look, I continued.

"One of the men was a cutter and the other a sewer. They were both from the old country and spoke with Yiddish accents. One day the sewer went missing."

The girl stopped crying. I had her attention.

"Exactly two weeks later, the sewer returned to the factory."

"Where did he go?" the girl asked.

"Well, that's exactly what the cutter wanted to know. So he says to the sewer, 'Where were you? You've been gone a long time.'"

I waited a few seconds, pretending to decide whether I should continue.

"What was his answer?" asked the girl.

"The sewer tells the cutter, 'I was in Africa.'"

"The cutter responds, 'What did you do in Africa?'"

"The sewer, while stitching a piece of cloth, says to the cutter, 'I traveled all over, I saw many things, and at the end of my trip, I was eaten by a lion.'"

"'Wait a second,' says the cutter. 'If you were eaten by a lion, you wouldn't be living.'

"The sewer looks around the factory and says, 'You call this living?'"

She may not have liked the story, but she appreciated the effort. She became my friend. Janie Fields.

Quickly, almost magically, there were other friends and then still others. Mostly because of Janie. She was likable, and, for whatever reason, she liked me.

What I came to realize is that in new surroundings, girls make quick decisions about who is pretty, smart, nerdy. Girls will attempt to mark other girls as their friends as quickly as possible on the theory that some girls, seeing that another girl has been marked, will move on. This process is best described as "spraying." An aggressive Italian girl, Maria (who would become my friend), was a first-class sprayer. Bringing a bottle of perfume to the first day of school, Maria actually doused the girls she wanted to meet.

In a new school, with new girls and boys who knew nothing about my past, I got sprayed.

THE DELICACY OF LOVE

"PLAY STREET" WAS the time set aside after lunch for exercise. The boys would occupy most of the gym, rocketing around or hurling a basketball or showing off martial arts moves they had observed in video games.

I usually ended up sitting in the bleachers with Maria and Janie.

Maria was pretty and funny, but short—one of our teachers actually called her a "little person," which Maria claimed was another way of saying "midget." The three of us hated athletics, so on those afternoons when we had Play Street, we would sit together and talk. Mostly about boys.

As we entered the gym one day, we noticed something new—a group of boys playing leapfrog. Leapfrog is when boys—who, as a group, are not especially concerned with hygiene—crouch on the ground while other boys, spreading their legs, vault over them; more often than not the bottom parts of the leaping boys are wiped across the heads of those crouching.

"*Animali!*" Maria snorted. "Adam would never do that."

Adam was Maria's big crush. His blue eyes were permanently covered by his then-popular Bieber cut. His smile always seemed too big for his face, and he had a big gap between his two front teeth. He was also a good shake taller than the other boys, and a lot taller than Maria. The Munchkins in *The Wizard of Oz* were a lot taller than Maria.

Sensitive to Maria's feeling for Adam, I hastily agreed.

"Adam. Of course not. No leapfrogging for that boy."

Janie nodded her head in mock solemnity. "Never."

We took a lap around the gym. Various people called out to Janie in greeting as we walked. Returning to the bleachers, we saw this:

Adam, squatting on the floor, his buttocks jutting in the air, readied himself as a short and chubby boy raced at him from behind. Before we could turn away, the other boy, his hands now up against Adam's behind, widened his legs and thrust himself upward.

But the laws of physics would not have it: the boy came down on Adam's head, which crashed to the floor and then disappeared.

"Where did he go?" I asked, opening my backpack to retrieve my daily chocolate bar.

Maria, stunned, said nothing. Her mouth wagged open.

Janie watched in silence, wary of Maria's next reaction.

"Do you hear anything?" I continued, unwrapping the chocolate.

It was then that I noticed a fringe of Adam's brown hair poking out from the other boy's crevice.

"Want a piece?" I offered, extending my candy bar.

Still nothing from Maria.

Janie looked away.

Maria never again spoke of Adam, never looked at Adam. While the boys in the gym could not leapfrog over Adam's great height, Maria had no such problem: she leapfrogged over his blue eyes, his shaggy hair, his unspeakable encounter with the other boy—and every other memory she had of him, or at least every imaginary encounter.

FRIENDSHIP AND CHOCOLATE

EVERYTHING ABOUT JANIE FIELDS was inoffensive. She wore the right things (circulation-squeezing jeans, bright graphic T-shirts paired with jelly bracelets called Silly Bandz), ate the right things (PB&J sandwiches with the crusts cut off), and had subscriptions to all the teen magazines. She had brown hair, brown eyes, and a medium build. She was an average student. And she was grating in a hard-to-identify way.

Because Janie was my friend, I took the time to study what was happening to her. I came to understand that it was going to happen anyway, and finally accepted it as a natural part of life, like butterflies burning in campfires or puberty.

Janie became a Popular Girl.

As Janie migrated to the other side, she spent less and less time with me and Maria. When it became clear that Janie was no longer our friend, Maria was hurt.

She started to pace, all four feet seven inches of her.

"Janie's embarrassed by me. She doesn't want to be seen with a midget."

There were, no doubt, a lot of bad things in Janie's character, but hating midgets wasn't one of them. Besides, there was a more obvious explanation.

"It's my personality," I offered matter-of-factly. "Janie needed me when she didn't know anyone else in the school, but now that she has other friends, she's ready to move on."

This was something I had come to understand. In my quest for friendship, I had developed the ability to repel people upon first serious conversation. Janie had lasted a surprisingly long time.

"I'm going to get her back for this," Maria declared.

One thing that could be said for the Rips family gene pool (a thing which, in my opinion, should have been drained years ago) is that we lack a thirst for revenge. It was why my father was more than happy to apologize to the tailor, and why I, listening to Maria, was thinking of nothing other than getting my daily chocolate bar from the local deli. My friendship with Janie was all but the faintest unpleasant aftertaste.

"Maria, it is my experience that if you let bad fortune alone for long enough it ripens into something amusing. A funny story, that sort of thing. Besides, a couple of our friends will stay with us."

"I'm going to kill her."

She wasn't listening.

"I have a plan," Maria continued.

"We go to the deli and get my candy bar?"

"No!"

"No?"

"We give her the Look."

"Okay. But first, let's go to the deli."

"No! First the Look, then the deli."

The message of the Look, also known as the evil eye, is something like: "Oh yeah? You think you're going to go and leave your friends? Well, you can bet that when you come crawling back to us, we're not even gonna look at you! Yeah, and we're gonna have a lot of fun without you! Ha!"

Maria and I needed to find Janie as quickly as possible so that we could deliver the Look and get to the deli before class started. We searched the school.

As soon as we caught sight of Janie's group, Maria started to speak out of the side of her mouth.

"*Uno, due, tre* . . . go!"

Nearing the center of Janie's posse, we began to strut and then, in unison, whipped our heads toward Janie, delivering the Look. But alas, Janie had turned away. We were giving the Look to the back of her head.

I figured this was the time to assert myself.

"Maria, I'm going to get my chocolate."

"Once more," Maria pleaded. "Then we can go."

"Maria, this has gone far enough. I need my chocolate!"

"Pleasssssse! You'll be my best friend."

Wasn't I already her best friend?

Back in formation, we marched toward the group.

"Uno, due, tre."

We snapped our heads. The Look.

Again, the back of Janie's head.

At this point, we could not stop. Over and over again, we marched, until we were doing nothing but circling Janie, snapping our heads and grunting. Rather undignified.

And I swear that Janie had a radar for the two of us, for every time we threw the Look, it missed.

The bell rang.

I was furious.

As Maria and I were leaving the cafeteria, I glanced back at Janie and to my horror noticed that Janie was now staring at us. But the horror came not from Janie's eyes but from her mouth. She was chewing what should have been mine. A chocolate bar.

GRETA RETURNS

THE FIRST FEW months of middle school went well. The change of environment had washed away my stench from elementary school, and though I'd lost Janie, I still had Maria and a couple other friends.

So here I was, the kid who, just a year before, no one wanted to have anything to do with, walking down the hallway with friends, greeting people at their lockers, and, best of all, going to birthday parties.

I was strolling into this happy reality one November morning when I caught sight of Maria and others crowded around a curly haired figure, who was, from nothing more than the top of her head, unmistakably Greta, my former friend from elementary school. Though she and I had ended up at the same middle school, because she hadn't been in Rebecca's class, I'd seen little of her.

Her friends were pretty, stylish, and involved in many school activities (dance, athletics, theater); mine were unattractive and liked anime. But to me, none of this mattered; my friends had the one quality that made them superior to anyone else at the school: they wanted to be with me.

"Nicki!" Maria greeted me, stepping away from the group surrounding Greta.

"Maria!" I responded, throwing my arms around her.

"You have to hear this," Maria whispered excitedly, pulling me into the group.

Greta had just begun the story.

"The other day . . ."

Greta dropped her voice. Everyone moved closer to hear.

". . . Oscar asked if I would meet him after school."

Oscar was a sweet, cute (though chinless), but not particularly smart boy. He was a friend of Greta's, and she had a crush on him.

"When we met, Oscar told me that he needed to tell me 'a secret.'"

Now we were getting to the good stuff.

"'Greta, I did something terrible,' Oscar told me, 'and I don't know what to do about it.'

"'There is nothing so bad that we can't handle it,' I said to Oscar. But I was worried. Oscar's parents were always busy and had no time for him. I was going to have to take charge."

Gad!

"So I said to Oscar, 'Oscar, you're going to have to tell me the secret. I can't help you, if you don't.'"

Don't do it, Oscar, my thoughts screamed.

But this wasn't going to happen. Greta had him and she wasn't letting go.

"It took me a few minutes to get it out of him," Greta continued. "But when he finally told me his secret, I thought to myself, Oscar's in trouble. Real trouble."

Greta went silent, shaking her head.

But how could the story end there? Greta had to tell us Oscar's secret. But even Greta, I was sure, wouldn't reveal Oscar's secret to a random crowd of girls.

Greta had already started up again.

"'Greta,' Oscar whispered to me, 'the problem is . . .'"

Greta raised her eyebrows, and then pointed to her stomach.

"*Diarrhea?*" Maria cried out.

Greta shook her head.

More confusion.

What?

Greta shoved her stomach outward.

Mother of Jesus. Oscar got someone pregnant!

None of us had heard anything like this. We shivered.

But Greta wasn't done, for she quickly made it clear that she knew the pregnant woman. We shouted out guesses.

A teacher?

A friend of Oscar's family?

Who could it be?

With each guess, Greta shook her head.

Tell us, Greta, tell us.

"Nicki, I'm sorry."

Did I just hear my name?

Everyone was staring at me.

The bell for first period rang. The girls raced to class.

I caught up with Greta.

"Greta, you just told them I'm pregnant!!"

"I said it was a '*dream*,' Nic. Didn't you hear that part?"

No one had heard "that part" because that was the part when she'd dropped her voice. Nothing I said in the following weeks could convince anyone that I, an eleven-year-old girl, wasn't carrying Oscar's child. Even Oscar, never too smart, seemed confused.

So while my fellow middle schoolers counted their school year in semesters, I counted mine in trimesters, for it wasn't until the third that anyone would believe that I hadn't done whatever a girl must do to get pregnant with someone like Oscar.

My fresh start had gone rotten.

MOVING ON

BY THE TIME I was in sixth grade, my parents had lived in the Chelsea for more than sixteen years. As an infant I hadn't taken up much space, but my presence in the apartment had grown. With each passing year, our home fit us a little more tightly, like a pair of my dad's college trousers. For this reason, my mom began to think about other places to live.

Every time she tried to introduce the subject, my dad would grumble. If we left the hotel, he'd argue, he would have to find new coffee shops, and that was quite a bit more disruption to his life than he was prepared to take on. We had plenty of space, he'd insist, failing to notice that it was impossible to move around without smacking into his bric-a-brac.

As much as I loved the Chelsea, the idea of moving was seductive. I was sick of people confusing my bedroom for a closet. This was an easy mistake given its small size. During my parents' many dinner parties people would inadvertently toss their coats on top of me while I slept. I could never manage more than one person in my room at a time without people sitting on my bed, which made playdates impossible. Fatigued by my constant pestering and my mother's unspoken but obvious irritation with the shared bathroom situation, my father gave in and announced one day that he had arranged for us to see a couple of apartments.

On Saturday afternoon, we put on our coats and headed out the door, down the elevator, and into the lobby. The Crafties were sitting in their usual spot and they applauded us as we walked by.

Mr. Crafty shouted after my dad, "Finally growing some cojones."

Smiley wheeled into the lobby and grabbed my mother. "Get out before they start stealing your detergent."

Stanley poked his head out from his office and waved to us.

As we walked, I thought to myself, "This is really happening; we are finally leaving the hotel."

Outside, my dad stopped walking, took a deep breath, and spun around to face the entrance, just as Stanley and Steve, the engineer who had worked at the hotel for decades, emerged from the entrance. Stanley seized my mom's hand and gave it a few vigorous pumps, then turned and did the same with my dad and me. After exchanging greetings, Stanley promptly showed us the way back inside the hotel.

Our first stop on Stanley's tour of vacancies took us to the seventh floor.

"You are going to love this one!" he said, directing his

excitement to my mother, for whom he had genuine affection. As we shuffled in to take a look, Stanley turned to my father and said, "You know . . . you're getting a good deal, these rents are below the Plaza." I had never had the pleasure of visiting that establishment, but I didn't think that visiting dignitaries would appreciate uneven floorboards, chipping paint, and a permanent malodor.

With each apartment, my parents murmured the appropriate "oohs and ahs" and asked Stanley and Steve the standard questions: do the fireplaces work (Stanley yes, Steve no), is it noisy (Stanley no, Steve yes), and who are the neighbors (Stanley, "an elderly artist and her invalid husband." Steve, "Crazies"—a raucous former inhabitant of a halfway house and the man she met there). My parents weren't bothered by any of this, and after a serious exchange with Stanley about taking the apartment, went off to examine the bedrooms and kitchen.

I might remind you that we didn't actually need to see the apartment: a floor above ours and in the same line, it was nearly identical.

As soon as my parents were far enough away, Steve confronted Stanley.

"Excuse me, Stanley, you realize that someone lives here? I think we should wait until David comes."

David was Stanley's son. He ran the day-to-day operations of the hotel, and it was understood that David would assume control when Stanley retired.

"Don't worry about David," Stanley replied, "he's not coming."

"Why?"

"I fired him."

"You fired David?" Steve's eyes bulged and his head jerked back. "Why?!"

"If you must know, I fired him because he said 'fuck you' to me. No one says 'fuck you' to me!"

"Are you kidding, Stanley?" I say 'fuck you' to you all the time."

"Okay, okay. But you're an exception."

"What about Artie? He says 'fuck you' to you every time you ask him for the rent. And Jerry and Nathan, they say 'fuck you' on a daily basis."

"That's right. Artie only says it when no one else is around, Jerry and I grew up together, and Nathan's too young to know better."

Nathan was the son of a bellman who had worked for Stanley's father.

"My rule is that you can only say 'fuck you' to me if you said it to me when I was a kid *or* if you are a kid *or* if nobody else is around. It's a three-part rule."

"I can say 'fuck you' to you?" I inquired.

They ignored me.

"So anyone can say 'fuck you' to you except David. Am I right?" Steve asked.

"If you keep this up, I'm going to fire you, too."

My dad wandered back into the living room, his head tilted

back to examine the ceiling sconces. "Excuse me, is there room service here?"

"No, Michael, you know that!" Stanley was getting flustered.

My dad considered this carefully, then shrugged. "Fair enough."

Steve, meanwhile, was heading out the door.

"Where are you going?" Stanley shouted after him.

"Fuck you, Stanley! Call David, tell him you're sorry, and get him to come back to work."

Stanley followed him, muttering under his breath.

My father turned to me. "I like this one."

"Me too," my mother shouted from the hallway. She was attempting to pry open the door to one of the bathrooms, when suddenly she stopped and stepped back.

A toilet flushed.

"Who's out there?" called a voice from inside.

My parents and I hoofed it back to our apartment.

KING OF THE NIGHT

AT THE HOTEL, I was spending a lot of time with Dahlia and her family. Visiting Dahlia and her mom one day, I noticed that Artie wasn't in his room. When he returned, he had difficulty talking. Dahlia and her mother were concerned.

Over the next months, Artie was required to take certain medicines, and though he would continue to drink from his flask (when Dahlia and her mother weren't home), he was limited as to what he could put in his mouth. But whatever problems he was having and however concerned others might be, he never seemed to worry.

In truth, Artie was not a guy who worried about much. For something to worry him meant that it was tougher than he was, and nothing was tougher than Artie.

One day when he could no longer speak, he went across the street to the art supply store and bought a small blackboard, and threw it around his neck. When he wanted to say something, he would scribble on the board in colored chalk. His speech became multicolored poetry.

When he slept, which he did a lot, Hammie would crawl onto his chest. I would sit next to them.

Soon people started dropping by the apartment. People I'd never seen before. Some of them caused a lot of talk in the building, so I guessed they were famous.

A few days after Artie died, Hammie died too.

A few days after that, this came out in *The New York Times*.

In the glittery, manic, often ostentatiously naughty 1970s and '80s, Arthur Weinstein was king of the night. His kingdom was a new breed of nightclubs that transcended disco balls, tired formulas and strobe lights to become ultra-hip destinations for those deemed worthy of entering. . . .

Mr. Weinstein opened illegal after-hours clubs downtown that mixed the fashionable and the young and artistic. The kids had radically odd colors of hair, and the coat-checker was a transvestite. . . .

Mr. Weinstein had another success with the World, a Lower East Side club—this one legal—distinguished by chandeliers, rotting rococo sofas, cherry syrup lights and a V.I.P. room where Stolichnaya—and perhaps other substances—flowed limitlessly. A former fashion photographer, he designed dazzling lighting systems for many other clubs, including the Limelight and the Tunnel. . . .

His wife, Colleen, said he died last Wednesday in Man-
hattan at the age of 60. The cause, she said, was head and
neck cancer. A friend, Steve Lewis, posted a message on the
Web saying Mr. Weinstein had died of "beauty."

When Dahlia and Colleen asked me if I wanted anything from Artie's belongings, I said no. I didn't need anything. I already had the obituary, folded and sticking out of my back pocket. Just like Artie.

THE STUDIO

AFTER SCHOOL, I often ended up at my mom's studio. While she was painting, I would sit on the floor and watch her fill pots with beeswax, melt it down, and then mix in pigments. She would pour the hot, colorful wax onto a wood panel, and create abstract patterns. If she didn't like the print, she would blowtorch the panel until it was smooth again. Many of the patterns were inspired by things she had seen on her travels to the most obscure and difficult parts of the world, such as Yemen, Syria, and Ethiopia. Her studio, like our apartment, was filled with curiosities that she had brought back from these places.

My mom had all kinds of art supplies, from watercolors to welding materials. Sometimes, I'd pull out a big pad of paper and start to draw. I would usually draw figures of pretty girls my age. Nothing special except for the fact that I liked these girls, and, more important, I made sure they liked me. My mom said she used to draw the same figures at my age.

In the studio one day, I noticed an African sculpture.

When I was a baby and would wake up early in the morning, my mother or father would take me outside. On the weekends, one of the few places open early was the flea market on Twenty-fifth Street and Sixth Avenue. It was housed in a two-level parking garage. Each floor was divided into booths, each one approximately the size of one parking space. Every weekend my parents and I would descend through the black plastic tarp that covered the entrance to the garage. On the other side, we were greeted by hundreds of people prepping tables and bargaining noisily. My parents would split off, one of them holding me, and wander around the treasures and the junk. One of my dad's favorite stands was filled with African sculptures, some so caked in mud, cloth, and shells that I couldn't tell whether they were human or animal, male or female.

My parents and I got to know the Malians who operated the stand, and a number of them would visit us in our apartment, sitting for hours drinking tea and talking about West Africa. One of them told me that these African objects were used to remind people of their link to places seen and unseen, the worlds of animals, ancestors, and gods.

The object in my mom's studio brought me relief, for I began to think that I was not stuck in the cage of what others thought of me. I was connected to worlds that had nothing to do with school—my mother and father and our relatives, yes, but also to the people in the Chelsea and to their lives and histories, real or imagined. I wanted to be the kid who would remind everyone else that they didn't have to stay in their cliques, for it seemed that even the most popular kids had conflicting thoughts about who they were.

I knew this because several of the same kids who ignored me when we were around other kids would approach me when we were alone. They found some comfort in telling me their problems, and I was happy just to be acknowledged.

Ana Penny, Greta's new best friend, was one such kid. She was slender and sweet with dark green eyes and strawberry blond hair; she could dance and sing, and she was always cast as the lead in the school musicals. She was (from the first day she stepped into nursery school to the day she would leave for college) adored.

Despite liking almost everyone, Ana could never bring herself to be friends with those whom her friends disliked. She bobbed up and down on the waves of other people's approval. And she hated herself for it, which made her tragic.

MY CROWD

MEREDITH PENNY, ANA's mother, made sure that nothing went wrong with her daughter's education. She did this by doing something which, for my parents, was unthinkable: she got involved in Ana's schools.

Meredith was a helicopter parent and hung out with those who were always involved with the school in some way: active in the PTA, raising money, organizing plays and musicals, always available to help other parents and teachers.

As a result of the influence she wielded, Meredith was able to guarantee that Ana was in the same classes as her friends with the best teachers in the school. The kids who had the misfortune to miss out on a parent like Meredith, and hadn't managed to make friends with one of their kids, ended up in classes taught by teachers who were nearing retirement, tenured and tired, and who were not yet looney enough to be fired.

We were the outcasts.

Within any social environment, there's a sort of pickup

game in which the captain of one team chooses her best friend, then the captain of the other team chooses hers, and then back and forth until the most desirable people have all been picked. There is nothing the undesirables can do but hope that they are not the last one picked.

It's one of the worst moments of anybody's life: you and some other unfortunate are the last two. One of you will be picked and the other will cry. The teacher says, "Hurry up! Just pick one!" and the captain gives in. "Fine . . . you," she says.

Your heart leaps as you start forward, smugly grinning (a piece of spinach lodged in your teeth) . . . until the captain corrects you. You're not the one; he chose the other kid, the one with the broken foot.

In my elementary and middle schools, the only ones I got to know were the last ones chosen—the ones brought to the bottom by the undertow of rejection. Mom likes to tell the story of when she asked me why a certain boy was being picked on. I replied, "He's a nerd." When Mom asked if I was one of the kids picking on the boy, I was astonished.

"Of course not. I'm a nerd too, and besides, he's a popular nerd."

If you wanted to meet us, the outcasts, it was not difficult. We all sat together in the middle school cafeteria. Table 17.

———

One of the kids at my table was Noah. He was a tall boy, who distinguished himself by sticking his head into other people's business—literally. Noah could not be within five feet of someone without feeling the need to touch his head against some part of their body.

Noah's habit was not taken well by the other students (or the teachers or the principal, who once found Noah wedged into his armpit), and people stopped talking to him. Soon parents attempted to have him removed from school. This seemed unfair, and I did what I could to keep him around.

One day, I took Noah aside. "Noah," I said, his head resting atop my shoulder, "try to imagine that everyone is surrounded by a bubble, and if you pop the bubble, something terrible will happen to the person inside."

Whether my little speech caused Noah to stop attaching his head to other people's bodies, I cannot say. But it stopped. And that, I thought, would be the end of it; the other kids would stop hating him, he wouldn't get kicked out of school, and I would have him off my back. A fine plan.

That was until Noah started licking people. I guess he thought that he could lick the bubble without popping it. From then on, he was "the Licker."

Horatio was another boy at my table. Smart and funny, he had close-cropped grayish brown hair and a head that was much wider at the chin than at the forehead. An egg.

In addition, he had a five-eleven frame, a distinguished belly, and a baritone. Taken together, Horatio was an imposing figure for a sixty-year-old man and a frightening one for a child.

The oddest thing about Horatio was that whenever he got agitated, which was often, he would lie facedown on the floor, stiff as a living body could be. No matter what people said or did to coax him off the ground, he would not budge until his anxiety passed, which could be ten minutes, twenty minutes, or more. No one, including Horatio, could predict how long he would be down there.

Nor did it matter where he was when he went down. It could be in the middle of class. Unable to answer a question, he would take his place on the floor, stiffen his body, and stay there until the bell rang. I once heard a teacher describe this as "social rigor mortis."

One day, my friend Maria was talking with Horatio, when she realized from the expression on his face that she might have hurt his feelings. "Horatio, don't plank! Please don't plank . . ." she started, but it was too late. Facedown on the floor, Horatio was gone.

Horatio, unsurprisingly, became known as "the Planker."

The Planker lived near me, and we would get off the subway together at Twenty-third Street. There were often two or three boys waiting for him outside the station, and they would chase him down the street. The Planker was usually able to get inside his building before they caught him, but when he couldn't, they'd jostle him around.

There was no reason for them to harm the Planker; they did it because they thought he was odd and vulnerable and their instincts and upbringing made them hate the weak.

Watching this day after day, it was easy to conclude that boys were much closer on the evolutionary map to orangutans than they were to girls.

One Friday, the Planker had promised to come with me to get cupcakes at Billy's (a local cupcakery), when he was rushed upon by the primates while exiting the subway. He fled with the boys in pursuit as I watched angrily. One does not gorge oneself on cupcakes alone. No, this annoyance had to be dealt with.

The next Monday after school I took one of the boys aside and told him that if he continued to chase the Planker, he would have to "reckon with me."

To my surprise, it worked.

Only years later did I learn that what scared them away was not my aggressive use of antique phrases, but my reputation (Greta loved to repeat the pool party story) for being homicidal. By the time it reached middle school, the story had twisted into:

"And then Nicolaia threw my little niece into the pool, and when my aunt cried out, Nicolaia pushed my aunt on top of the baby, screaming, 'You take that, motherf#@ker!'"

In addition to the Licker and the Planker at table 17, there was Maria. After being rejected by Janie and the incident with the Look, there was no one at the school who wanted to hang out with her, and she ended up at the table with the rest of us.

Maria was the one person who stuck with me through the

months in which I was not pregnant with Oscar's child. Maria had the biggest smile and a bigger heart.

The only other boy at the table was Joshua. He was the Planker's best friend, but unlike the Planker, who was a long fellow, Joshua was barely taller than Maria. But what Joshua lacked in height, he made up for in sarcasm.

My first encounter with Joshua was in the school gymnasium, where he lay on the ground, moaning and frothing. His head swiveled back and forth, cleaning up the loose dirt on the floor.

By the time the nurse arrived (a good twenty minutes after the attack), Joshua was still moaning and frothing. Witnesses helped the nurse diagnose Joshua with a case of made-a-snarky-remark-and-got-kicked-in-the-gonads disease.

We, however, came to appreciate Joshua's capacity to weep. That boy could weep in response to events that hardly bothered anyone else; he could weep loudly or softly, day or night, and always in earnest.

Scattered among the other kids, we had a fighting chance of pulling ourselves up to the middle of the social ladder, or at least to another rung. Grouped together at one table, we were finished: no one could look at me without thinking of the Planker, or look at Maria without being reminded that the girl next to her had attempted to drown a baby.

But in my mind we were a club of superheroes: Joshua had the power to flood cities with his tears; Noah's tongue could deafen or strangle enemies; Horatio could make a speedy escape by lying on the floor; and Maria, small, could sneak up on people without them ever knowing it. I, though, had the greatest power of all: the ability to alienate people who had just met me.

Try as I might, I could not fight off my fondness for this gang and came to see myself as their protector—a sort of Professor X or Nick Fury, the mother of them all.

THE SCHNOZ

A BOY CAME to my middle school from a foreign country.

He was tall and well-built and spoke with an accent. His parents, who were very well off (a villa in Malta; summers sailing the Mediterranean), wanted their son to experience New York. That boy, to my astonishment, had no interest in the girls everyone else liked; he wanted a girl who had the substance to sustain them through their long romance. In short, he chose me.

And that is how my life turned around.

Well, that is how my life would have turned around had this been anything other than one of several stories in my vibrant cloud of fantasies.

So it was with some interest that I took notice when word spread around the middle school that a good-looking foreign boy had been seen in the principal's office. His father was the head of a big company and had decided to bring his family to New York for a couple years.

Roberto, the boy, had a very long and thin nose. But this nose did not detract from his face: it had its own existence, entirely disconnected from the boy himself—a weather vane spinning happily while the rest of the house went on about its business.

I first met the Schnoz in the school cafeteria. He was surrounded by a crowd of girls. But he was not staring over the crowd of blond heads to find me, the one girl who would give him a long and happy life. No, he was thrilled with the attention of the other girls, and as the weeks passed, he was seen with many of them, sometimes two or three at a time, making them laugh with his accent and crazy gestures and funny stories.

Almost one month after he'd entered the school, he was dating Penelope Brewster. I can't even believe that her name is on the pages of my chronicle. But there it is.

Penelope Brewster was the J. Lo of my middle school. One of the few girls with a postpubescent body, she flaunted her A-cups—the only A's she would ever receive.

Her speckled green eyes were carefully rimmed in midnight-blue eyeliner, and her bubblegum-pink lips were always curved in a signature smirk. It bumped up your social standing just to be seen next to her, and if she knew your name, you were raised even higher. She once sneezed on the Planker, and he was immediately surrounded by a group of jealous boys. No matter what she did, it was worshipfully received.

If an arrow were shot through the hearts of the most venomous and beautiful women in history, it would surely pierce Penelope Brewster.

———

The Schnoz was assigned to my English class, where he was surrounded by Penelope and her friends. One day in class, the teacher announced the names of those who had been selected for the school musical. They were Meredith Penny's selections, and those were as predictable as indigestion after Passover dinner: Ana Penny (Meredith's daughter), Penelope Brewster, and their entourage.

The Schnoz was evidently surprised that the musical was being cast exclusively with his girlfriend and her tone-deaf friends, for he cried out:

"The slooots?"

The teacher turned to him.

"Excuse me, Roberto?"

"You know . . . a slooots," the Schnoz repeated.

She did not know; nor did anyone else.

"A slooots is a . . . a . . ." He was having trouble finding the words.

"Exactly what are you trying to say, Roberto?" the teacher insisted.

Everyone was now staring at him.

Suddenly his arms shot forward. Grabbing what appeared to be an imaginary figure, he began frantically jackrabbiting his pelvis back and forth.

"*Roberto,*" exclaimed the teacher.

I jumped in.

"I believe that what our friend and recent immigrant Roberto is trying to say is 'slut' . . . which, if I'm not mistaken, is a woman who . . ."

"Ms. Rips, that is enough."

But I would not be denied.

"If Roberto were speaking in his own language, he would have used the word *puta.*"

"*Si! Puta!*" cried the Schnoz, joyfully.

"That," I added, "would be spelled *p-u—*"

"*PUTA! PUTA!*" exclaimed the Schnoz, high-fiving the puzzled boys around him.

Our teacher would endure no more.

"Class is over!"

"*t* . . . that stands for . . ." I continued.

"Ms. Rips, I shall see you and Roberto after class."

But the worst of it did not come after class. No, the "t" for trouble came much later, as word spread of what the Schnoz had said in English class. Penelope Brewster did not appreciate having her boyfriend describe her as a "slooot," and he would have to be punished. And nothing the Schnoz said could change her mind.

But ending her romance with the Schnoz, which she did in the lunchroom to make certain everyone knew, was not enough. The Schnoz, who was still confused by what was happening to him, had to be banished from all things popular, and Penelope's friends were happy to oblige.

The Schnoz was in popularity free fall. How far and brutal the plunge was revealed only when the Schnoz, after tumbling from one table to another in the lunchroom, landed dazed at table 17, the table of losers, cripples, and malcontents.

My table.

MOM VS. MAMA

MY SCHOOL INSISTED that phones and computers be stored in lockers before classes began and retrieved at the end of the day. Violators were treated severely, so all of us obeyed.

After a long day of wading through the educational and social mire, I returned to my locker to find it swinging on its hinges. Panicked, I shuffled through its contents (three chocolate bars, a bag of cookies, a sweater) to find that my phone was gone.

As soon as I reached home, I told my mom. She asked whether I'd reported it to the principal. I hadn't.

She did.

Mom has a lot going on in her mind, which means that she is not always paying attention. So when she does, it's startling—like something dropping out of the rafters onto your dinner plate.

That was the case here. I saw it in her eyes. She was going to find the person who stole my phone.

Everything told me that it was a bad idea.

"Mom, let it go. It was an old phone."

Mom hated cowardice and she smelled it here. Now there was no thought of her turning back; she needed to set an example for her daughter.

I, on the other hand, needed someone to convince her to abandon her mission—someone who was willing to run from a minor skirmish, who always had at hand the most convincing excuses for avoiding a fight; someone who feared paper cuts as others shy from shotguns.

I needed my father, a self-described "descendant of quitters and quislings."

But he was not around, and Mom was already speaking to someone at the phone company.

With the information she was given, she began to sleuth about, disguising her voice on one call, pretending to be conducting a survey on another, and then (to my amazement) she was on the phone, speaking French, with someone who was connecting her to their "associate" in Barbados.

My mother got the fellow in Barbados to mention that he had a niece who went to school in New York City. That niece, my mother deduced, had my phone.

Mom reported the girl's name to the principal. The principal gave the name to the police.

A few days later, the police reported that the kid who took

my phone was not using it herself, but had stolen it for one of her uncles. The girl and her mother were called to meet with the police and officials at the school.

The girl, as my luck would have it, was in a group at the school who were led by "Mama," an older girl with bulging muscles. Mama did not like the fact that one of her own was in trouble, and from that moment on, I was in trouble.

Girls shoved me in the hall, pushed me down a staircase, and threatened to hurt me. I also feared that the girl's uncle would come after me.

At a meeting with the principal, Mom threatened to pull me out of school, but the principal agreed to assign a counselor to accompany the girl between classes and to sit with her at lunch. The counselor would attempt to talk through whatever had caused the girl to break into my locker.

Mama and her gang followed them around the school, attempting to intimidate the counselor. If the counselor left to go to the bathroom, Mama, the girl, or one of their gang would come over to where I was sitting and bang on the table, yelling obscenities.

The principal offered me his personal assurance that everything was under control: Mama and her gang, the relative and his men, could not harm me. I had, according to the principal, nothing to worry about. He would make sure that I was protected.

It did not take me long to figure out the principal's plan, though when I confronted him, he denied it: have me secretly followed at school by a portly fifty-year-old—a man, who, attempting to be inconspicuous (ducking in and out of classrooms, bathrooms, and closets), disguised himself by regularly changing his outfits and hair color.

As the days passed, the man reached ever deeper into his closet and medicine cabinet. Each week, his costume regressed five or six years and his hair turned noticeably darker, which, after not so long, brought him dangerously close to the style and hair color he had when, many pounds lighter, he himself was in middle school.

My mom was not happy with all of this, so she, being my real protector, came to school every day to make sure that nothing horrible happened.

If there is one helpful observation I might share, it is this: if you are trying to find a boyfriend or just a friend, it does not help to have your mother, along with a fifty-five-year-old man dressed in rare clothing and smelling rarer, following you around the hallways.

Several weeks into this, I was headed down the fourth-floor hallway, followed by Mr. Bean and Mom, when I noticed a group of people coming in the opposite direction. It was the girl who stole my phone, followed by the school counselor, followed by Mama, followed by Mama's gang.

The girl and I stopped.

We exchanged glances as our entourages glared at each other. Suddenly she smiled, perhaps at how ridiculous it all seemed. I smiled back. The feud was over.

THE DANCE

THERE WERE TWO places where popular kids gathered outside of school and to which I was desperate to be invited: parties at a classmate's apartment and a weekly soccer game.

The game was held on a field far from school in order to make certain that kids like me did not wander by accidentally. The girls would sit on the sideline talking while their boyfriends ran around kicking the ball.

My chances of getting invited to either were zero.

Some high school kids came up with the idea of throwing social events for kids like me. They sent out mass invitations on Facebook announcing dance parties for a "select group of people," giving the invitees the opportunity to meet "others like themselves." What was not said was that the "select group" were those who could not get invited to a normal party and the "others like themselves" were other unfortunates.

The topper was that we had to pay to attend the event.

The kids who organized the party were in it for the profit, and given how desperate we all were, we did not hesitate to pay.

The truth is that, though I would have been happy to attend as many of these as possible, my father was against it. As a result, I only went to one.

The party was at a loft in SoHo, a part of town known for its old factory buildings. When the factories moved out, artists moved in. When developers drove the artists out, the area filled with expensive apartments and chain stores. Some of the old factory spaces have been renovated and are rented for weddings, graduation events, and parties for losers.

At the party, I recognized a number of kids whom I had not seen since elementary school. They had been unpopular then and were, like myself, still unpopular. A certain embarrassed bonding ensued.

I was having a fine time until, halfway through the evening, I ran into the last person I would have expected to see at the event—Uhura. The few times I had run into Uhura since elementary school, he had always had the upper hand—finding the cleverest ways of reminding me, and anyone else around us, of my grade school crush on him and the fact that he (broodingly attractive and desirable) had wanted nothing to do with me.

In our most recent encounters, he had added the suggestion that I was stalking him.

But now I had him: only pathetic kids came to these parties; Uhura was at the party; therefore, Uhura was . . .

I didn't need to complete the logic. He knew, and it was the reason that, having spotted me moving toward him, he was now headed quickly in the opposite direction.

"Oh, Harry," I sung out.

He stopped and turned.

"Nice to see you, Harry. I hadn't expected . . ."

But Harry was smart, and in those few seconds between the "Oh, Harry" and "Nice to see you," he had readied an efficient and brutal response.

"Nicolaia," he said, "I have a girlfriend. And you?"

I was knocked against the ropes.

I jabbed back weakly: "I have a boyfriend."

That stopped him.

"Who is he?" Skepticism glistened on his lips.

I hadn't anticipated that one.

"He's tall."

Uhura was short, so I knew that stung.

"And handsome," I punched again before he could recover.

"Do I know him?" Uhura countered.

"No. He's new to the city. A foreigner with . . . uhmm . . . sandy hair and green eyes . . ."

This was Build-a-Boyfriend Workshop.

"There was trouble in his country," I continued, beginning to enjoy myself. "He and his family had to escape."

"They lost everything?"

I had to end it.

"Just Grandma."

I dropped my head, pretending I was too upset to continue.

Had Uhura a jot of humanity, the questioning would have stopped there.

"What about her husband?" he asked, searching for an opening in which to throw his fist. "Did he come to America?"

"Grandpa? Right. Yes and no."

"Yes *and* no?"

"He died on the boat."

"Of what?"

Heartbreak? No. Too sentimental. Seasickness? Obviously not.

I needed something quick. Otherwise, everything would come undone.

"Myasthenia gravis."

A voice from the darkness. Was I hearing things?

If it was someone, it could only be a person who had known me and my pretend illness and was also smart enough to remember a Latin phrase that she'd heard only once, years before.

"Harry! Nicolaia!"

The voice again.

Uhura and I turned around.

It was the one person in the universe more distasteful to Uhura than me. The person responsible for sending an entire class of eleven-year-olds, including Uhura, to schools at the other end of the galaxy. And there she was—the evil genius herself.

Fan.

Was I ever happier to see anyone?—certainly no one so disturbed. But she glided away before we could speak.

I turned to Uhura. He too was gone. Outnumbered by his enemies, he had beamed himself back to the starship.

THE SHAMAN

THERE WERE THREE problems with the dances at my school, and not one had a solution or, at least, not one I could figure out.

The first was that most of the kids at my school were girls, which meant that a lot of time was spent dancing with other girls.

The second was the hygiene of the boys.

Despite certain problems I had with rhythm and my earlier experience with Pippi, I really enjoyed dancing, and the class I most looked forward to in seventh grade was ballroom dancing. My fantasies included Sleeping Beauty and Prince Phillip gliding around the forest, their fingertips touching, his hand gently guiding her minuscule waist. Prince Phillip smelled permanently of Febreze. It turned out to be nothing like I'd imagined; unenjoyable and awkward. I had always suspected that boys were unclean (leapfrog), but now, in such close proximity to their sweaty, nervous bodies, my fears were confirmed. The boys in my class and I were like two boats passing in the night—except that one boat had terrible night vision and kept steering into, and sweating on, the first boat at inopportune times. One of my teachers regularly shouted out at the boys: "It's called deodorant!" These same boys had a tendency to stare at, well, as the same teacher put it, "Her eyes are up here."

Into the center of this dropped Ned Frisco—the third unsolvable problem.

Ned, who had transferred from another school, was the nephew of the crossing guard, Krysta, one of the most reviled people at the school. Krysta stood on the corner of the street and screamed at those who crossed without her permission. It made no difference whether you were a student, parent, or teacher. You had to ask Krysta before crossing.

What's more, Krysta's decision to usher you across had nothing to do with the traffic. The street could be empty and Krysta would force you to wait for her word. She could often be cruel.

The first thing we noticed about her nephew, Ned, was that he had a beard. It stretched from the bottom of his overgrown Elvis sideburns to the middle of the wobbly thickness that was his chin and then back up the other side. A thing of alien beauty.

One last thing about Ned. He believed himself to be irresistible to females. All females. No one was beyond his advances—classmates, obviously, but teachers and mothers as well.

The place he proved most adventurous was on the dance

floor. There were already too few boys in the ballroom dance class, and Ned Frisco made a point of dancing with every girl. He was impossible to avoid. We all waltzed, fox-trotted, and tangoed with him, one hand firmly grasping our nose to avoid the odors from whatever was fermenting in his beard and the other swatting at his hand as it traveled farther than necessary down our backs.

After class one day, as I was doing my best to engage a cute boy in conversation, Ned walked up to me, winked, snapped his stretchy pants, and said, "I'm glad my auntie didn't see us on the dance floor," implying that he and I had been doing something we shouldn't have been.

Another time I was standing with a small group of girls when he came up, tugged his pants up over his great girth, and announced, "If any of you need a dance partner, *caballero* Frisco is available."

Stop. I forgot to mention that Ned had man boobs, which made him all the more interesting. I wondered why Ned stared at the breasts of girls in my class when he had a perfectly respectable pair of his own. Ned's breasts were some of the most developed in our grade and were often looked at with longing by followers of Penelope Brewster.

The boys in the class had a different reaction to Ned. To them, he embodied something they had only glimpsed from afar—manhood. With his suave manner (the snapping of his stretchy pants and suggestive remarks) and his beard, Ned Frisco was a shaman of sexuality.

Boys consulted him, gave him gifts, showed him their pizzles, all in the hope that he'd allow them into the kingdom of maleness. But it always ended with a shake of Ned's head. None of the boys were allowed to cross over. Adulthood, though attractive to those who are constantly told to "wait until you're older," was not a venture any of us were ready for. Ned Frisco guarded the gateway to our side of innocence, and knew none were ready for the frustration growing up had to offer.

In that way he was much kinder than his aunt.

In the meanwhile, I was coming to the conclusion that dance and I should find different partners.

TIC-TAC-TOKE

ONE GRIM DAY, as I was entering the subway, still smoldering from gym class, my oversized book bag around my shoulders, trying to push back ugly thoughts about the waves of humanity around me, I felt a tug on my pack.

Greta. Hair perfect despite the humidity, carrying nothing, her face bright and undisturbed by the subway at rush hour.

"Nic, where are you going?"

She knew exactly where I was going: Twenty-third Street, where I would exit and walk half a block west to the place where I lived—actually, just next door to the place where Greta lived. It was the same route we took every day.

The only difference was that today Greta was speaking to me.

"Nicolaia, I thought we should catch up. We haven't talked in ages."

Come to think of it, Greta, you're right, I thought. When was the last time we talked? Oh yes, now I remember: *it was when you announced that I was pregnant!*

"As you may know, Nicolaia, I have a boyfriend."

As you may know? The two of them were never apart, and Greta made certain that everyone at school understood that they were boyfriend and girlfriend. They were the cutest couple in the school.

"Well, Nicolaia, something is happening with Joseph that is very disturbing."

Trouble in Cuteville?

"Greta, I'm not sure I'm the best person to talk to. I've never had a boyfriend."

"You're an old . . . friend. You know me. You would tell me if I'm boring, or losing my looks, or if . . . he's going out with someone else."

A single, perfect tear was on its way down Greta's cheeks, and when Greta cried, nothing could stop me or anyone else from doing what Greta wanted.

"Okay, Greta. What happened?"

"When we first started dating, he wanted to do things with me—go to the movies, hang in the park, listen to music. Now when we're together, he watches videos and sleeps. I can't get him to do anything. Be honest with me, Nicki."

Contrary to my previous denial, I knew something about Greta's problem, though I wasn't sure what to do about it.

A few months before, I had entered my social studies class and discovered that a boy was occupying my seat in the second row. With my eyesight less than it should be (which may or may not have been a side effect from the months I spent partaking in optical testing), I needed to be close to the front, so this was unacceptable.

The boy refused to move. With class starting and my pleas going nowhere, I took the last vacant seat in the room.

It was only after sitting down that I noticed a strange odor. When it became clear that the odor was not passing, I leaned toward the boy on my right.

"What is that odor?"

He looked confused.

I asked him again.

He turned to me.

"I don't want any cookies today," he announced.

I turned to the boy on my left and posed the same question. He stared at me for a few seconds and put his head down on the desk.

At lunch, the others at table 17 tried their best not to sit next to me, and I realized that I'd transported a small, but still horrible, part of the odor to the lunch table. I was now the outcast of outcasts.

I explained that I'd been forced to move chairs in social studies and was now in a part of the class where everything smelled bad. When I was finished, Horatio the Planker spoke.

"You, my odoriferous friend, are in the Stoner Corner."

"What?"

"Those fellows in your class meet every morning, have a smoke with their OJ and cereal, and then go off to class. Over lunch, they have another smoke, followed by food, lots of food. There are at least a couple of them in every class, and teachers let them do whatever they want so long as they don't bother anyone."

"So what's the odor?"

"You really are naïve. Now, if you don't mind, it's that time of day."

"Horatio, no, I have more questions."

But he was already planking.

With each day, the odor in the Stoner Corner was less offensive, like when an anthropologist, having finally deciphered the spitting rituals of a tribe, is no longer bothered by the clots of saliva decorating his trousers. And the stoners, sensing that I knew their secret, seemed friendlier.

One day, sitting in social studies, squinting at the board, I received a poke in the ribs from a resident of the Stoner Corner.

"Do you play tic-tac-toe?"

A trick question?

"I haven't played in some time," I said, "but I'm pretty sure it'll come back to me."

"Well, you're going to have to be good because we practice every day."

He may have sensed concern in my face, for he volunteered a piece of advice.

"Don't play Dale. He's the best."

I turned toward Dale, who, from the size of the puddle

gathering next to his mouth on the desk, had been napping for most of class.

"Thanks. I'll keep that in mind."

When I described my conversation about the tic-tac-toe game to Horatio, he remarked that if I really wanted to understand what was going on inside the heads of these gentlemen, I needed to play tic-tac-toe with them.

It was not as if I hadn't thought of this; the problem was, as I'd foolishly explained to Horatio, if I played and lost, I would never recover my pride. With this, Horatio rose from his chair.

I knew what was coming and did not like it: when not planking, Horatio was given to delivering speeches. Why? I don't know, but it was always infuriating, since what one expected to be a personal exchange could suddenly turn very public.

"Fellow members of the lunchroom . . . [long pause as he gazed around] . . . let us assume, for the purpose of this speech, that Nicolaia has pride."

For all of his oddity, he was not without insight. But he could be so insulting.

"And let us further assume," he continued, "that her pride is worth saving."

What did I tell you.

I left the lunchroom.

Later that day, as I made my way to my seat in social studies, I sensed a change in the atmosphere. One of the boys, Tim, tapped me on the shoulder.

He spoke quietly. "It's time."

I gulped. He pointed to my opponent, Jeremy, a burly stoner who played the drums.

"Ready your paper, get out your pens, we will let the newbie go first."

I decided my safest course of action would be to put an "X" in the center. It was now Jeremy's turn.

Jeremy stared at me. Jeremy fidgeted. Jeremy cracked his knuckles. Jeremy let out a grunt. Jeremy picked up his pen. Jeremy put down his pen.

The bell rang.

Jeremy turned to me.

"I want a rematch."

He then collected his notebooks and left the class.

I turned to Tim, the referee. He looked at me in awe.

"Whoa, maybe you should play Dale."

I headed to lunch and sat down next to Horatio.

"Horatio, I don't think they've ever finished a game."

He nodded his most superior nod.

"Of course not."

Thus, I came to know the members of the Stoner Corner, and there were several whom I liked. They were never alert enough to have a full conversation, or tic-tac-toe match for that matter, but we would have short exchanges, and there were things I came to learn about them, one of which was that they included among their sleepy society a fellow with long bangs and a longer name—Joseph Eliot McCormick Potter— or, as he was better known, "Greta's boyfriend."

By telling Greta that her boyfriend was a stoner, I would give her comfort or, at least, release her from the fear that she had become uninteresting or, worse, no longer cute.

But was I the one to tell her? The stoners were a secret group, and they'd allowed me the privilege of peeking into their clubhouse. Besides, if Joseph Eliot McCormick Potter had wanted Greta to know what he was up to, he would have told her.

I decided to keep my mouth shut. But as I walked away from my conversation with Greta, I heard a swell of whimpering.

I turned around.

"Greta. Do you know how to play tic-tac-toe?"

She paused, feigning reflection, her index finger now laid against her cheek.

"I haven't played in a long time, but . . ."

I remembered why she and I had been friends.

"Greta, you might ask Joseph if he wants to play. It might keep him awake and away from videos. And from there, who knows . . ."

After that, there was no more Greta retelling the baby-in-the-pool story, no more pregnant Nicolaia dreams, no more I-am-cuter-than-you attitude. In short, Greta was grateful.

SUMMER CAMP

ONE AFTERNOON, AFTER school, I put Cream Puff in her ball and took her out into the hallway of the hotel. After thirty minutes or so, I went to help my mother with something in the apartment, leaving Cream Puff behind. When I returned minutes later, there was no Cream Puff and no hamster ball.

I was confused but also frightened: the door between the hallway and the rest of the hotel was closed, as were all of the rooms on the floor, and there was no vent or other place in the hallway into which Cream Puff and her ball could have disappeared.

I called to Mom, and the two of us began to knock on doors. In one of the apartments lived a middle-aged woman whose apartment was filled with hundreds of shiny glass objects—vases, paperweights, mirrors, and chandeliers.

She dressed in vintage clothing and had the manner of a child: with her pageboy haircut, dyed nightmarish black, she skipped, never walked, and spoke in a high-pitched whine.

When asked about Cream Puff, she claimed that she'd just returned home and had seen nothing.

When we had asked every neighbor on the floor, Mom and I opened the door between our hallway and the main stairway.

At the bottom, six floors below, was Cream Puff, framed in the shards of her ball.

I believe that the woman-child across the hallway had opened the door to the staircase, purposely allowing my hamster to roll to his death. She resented Cream Puff. She, unlike Cream Puff, could never get her shiny ball spinning fast enough to make herself happy.

———

Because of what had happened to Cream Puff, Mom began to look for a summer camp that would give me a chance to spend time with animals.

After a great deal of research, she found the perfect camp: not only was its focus on teaching kids to care for animals, but it was in the Ozarks, not far from my maternal grandmother's home in St. Louis. The plan was for me to spend a few days in St. Louis and then depart for two weeks at Camp Maximilian.

Maria's parents, who would soon return their family to Italy, thought that Camp Maximilian would be a great way for their daughter to experience America, and signed her up to join me.

Maria and I spent hours talking about camp: our wardrobes—crop tops, multiple floral skirts, skinny jeans, ballet flats for day wear, party dresses and heels for evening—and, of course, the boys we would meet, all tall, strong, well-mannered; in short, nothing like the boys we knew at school.

Months later, we were off. After two days in a television-induced vegetative state at my grandmother's, Maria and I boarded the bus to camp. As we rode through what my grandmother called "*Deliverance* country," we began to feel a burgeoning sensation in the pit of our stomachs. For Maria it was excitement. I, however, found myself holed up in the tiny bus bathroom. When we arrived, I rallied ho and raced with Maria to our cabin, where she and I claimed the bunk farthest from the bathroom. The Winter Valley experience had taught me that much.

We didn't have much time to settle in before we were called to the assembly where we would be assigned our animals. The idea behind the camp was that each of us would pick an animal, and from the first day to the last we would be responsible for everything having to do with it.

And what a range of animals there were! Sheep, parrots, snakes, chimps, bush babies, scorpions, and llamas. The list of animals had been distributed before we arrived at camp, and I'd chosen a lemur. Maria had picked a wallaby.

True to the camp's promise, I was introduced to my lemur that first day. His name was King Julius. He was overweight with big bug eyes and a white patch on his head.

The next day I would begin to receive my instructions on how to care for him. That night, my dreams were filled with images of King Julius and me walking through the fields, his tiny monkey-like hand clasping mine.

———

Our first morning at Camp Maximilian began with a breakfast of pancakes, eggs, grits, and sausage; just the sort of food I loved. As soon as we finished, Maria and I raced to the area where the animals were kept.

Calling our names, the counselor pointed to the buildings where our lessons in animal husbandry would begin. Mine was white, with green shingles and ivy. Plain and sweet.

Inside the cottage I noticed a crowd of people standing around a table. A man left the group and greeted me at the door.

"Nicolaia," he called out.

"Yes."

"I am the director of the camp."

We shook hands.

"Your animal is King Julius?"

I nodded and started to tell the director how happy I was to be there, to meet him, and to spend time with King Julius.

He cut me off, pulling me toward the table where others were standing.

"Not right now. We need to remove King Julius's testicles."

It took a second or two for this to sink in, but it was just long enough for me to exchange glances with King Julius, who gave me the look that Christ gave Judas, Sirius Black gave

Peter Pettigrew. King Julius had obviously not been consulted on whether he needed his testicles removed.

Lathered on top of this was the fright of the operation. The syringes and scalpels, the white gowns and lights, King Julius clamped on a metal table. I spent the next fifteen minutes handing the vet in charge different tools as he snipped important bits away from King Julius.

It was quickly apparent that my dear mother, undoubtedly distracted when she scanned through the list of camps, had picked one intended for junior veterinarians. Which is to say that the camp's population (with the exception of Maria, myself, and King Julius) was less interested in the emotional give and take between man and animal than in taking animals apart and putting them back together again.

I was still suffering from the feeling that I was responsible for Cream Puff's death. With King Julius's trauma now weighing on me too, I was feeling pretty down.

After a few days, though, King Julius, still laid up but less testy, was willing to consider me his friend. And he proved to be a fine friend.

Every morning I would come and sit in the room, which he shared with two other lemurs, and feed him pieces of banana, which he would nibble off of my finger. I would talk to him about my life and the Chelsea Hotel, which I missed. It was especially hard to be away from the Crafties, to whom I confided everything (much, no doubt, to their annoyance). King Julius would gibber back in lemur language. Sometimes I would adjust his bandages or bring him toys I had made out of toilet paper rolls and string.

On the weekends Maria and I signed up for various classes. One of those was Goat Feeding. We imagined prancing in Dorothy-esque dresses with baskets of goat food tucked under our arms, flinging the feed into the air as the goats danced at our feet.

Twelve of us arrived at the barn early the first morning. The goat-feeding session was led by a bubbly counselor in training who introduced herself as Daisy.

Daisy started passing around a stack of papers.

"I need y'all to sign these and return 'em right now."

She twirled her ringlets. Daisy was used to being cute.

As the papers were being distributed, Daisy began to recite the different types of goat feed and what went into them.

"Chaffhaye, clover, alfalfa, grass . . ."

A tiny boy in the front raised his hand.

"Excuse me, Miss Daisy?"

"Yes."

"Why do we have to sign this?"

Daisy's cute began to blacken.

"Why, honey, in case you get hurt."

"I am only eleven years old, I don't think I can sign things," the little kid insisted.

Daisy had already returned to the feed list.

"Oats, wildflower honey, urea . . ."

What did she say?

"Buddy up!" Daisy hollered, ushering us inside the barn.

As we marched past, Daisy forced our sleeves up to our shoulders.

The barn was dark inside. In the middle of it were two large vats, one filled with an amber liquid and the other with a mixture of oats. Daisy grabbed the nearest camper, dipped her arms into the amber liquid—honey—then into the feed.

Daisy did this with each of us, and when she was finished, we stood there, arms perpendicular to our bodies, dripping with honey and goat feed.

She opened another door leading to the outdoor goat pen.

"Walk two-by-two through the pen," Daisy shouted. "In a nice straight line."

Miss Clavel?

"Arms out straight. And don't come out until all the goats are fed! Bye now."

The door closed behind us.

As our eyes adjusted to the sun, we discovered that we were standing directly before forty ill-tempered goats.

The goats moved toward us and began to nibble and slurp at our arms. We were all too scared to move. Some of us began to tremble.

It was not very long before the boy who'd asked about the papers panicked, bolting toward the wall of the pen.

Anarchy.

We ran around as the goats butted us and nipped at our

arms. I could hear Maria pounding at the door to the barn, begging Daisy to free us.

Racing toward Maria, a goat bleating at my heels, I hauled her under my arm and broke toward a bush at the corner of the pen.

We dove into the bush, just ahead of the goat.

"Well, this was unexpected," I said to Maria.

No response from Maria.

I turned around.

She was licking her arms.

Holy mother.

She extended one of her arms toward me.

"Molto delizioso!"

I shook my head in disbelief.

"Really?" she questioned. "Wildflower honey and oats."

There was no convincing me.

Maria seemed offended.

"And what do *we* get at this camp?! Cheeses and mac— *disgustoso.*"

"Urea, Maria." I felt obligated to mention this as a possible ingredient in the goat feed.

"Who's that?"

The door to the pen opened. Daisy.

"What did you think of our goats?" she asked cheerily.

We swarmed passed her. Maria looked back.

"Vado a mangiare il damn capre!"

Which, as Marie explained it later, meant that given half a chance, she would eat Daisy's damn goats.

The boys at camp were nothing like what we had imagined.

What they lacked in sophistication, they made up for with other talents. Such a boy was Jimmy Robbins, whom Maria and I befriended in baking class. Jimmy looked like the love child of Robert Downey Jr. and a gorilla.

Maria and I signed up for all the baking classes because they were really more like eating classes. We would sit and chat as the teacher cooked food. It was perfect. As with most classes, the boys immediately claimed one side of the room, the girls the other.

We encountered Jimmy when we heard a commotion from across the room. Needing only the smallest excuse to visit the boys, we rushed over.

Jimmy was standing in the center of a small group. Next to him was his best friend. Half Jimmy's size, he was known as "Half-Jimmy."

Half-Jimmy was holding a roll of brown paper towels—the sort one finds in a gas station bathroom.

Jimmy addressed his namesake (well, half namesake): "Half-Jimmy, I'm ready."

Half-Jimmy grabbed Full Jimmy.

"You don't have to do this, Jimmy."

"I must," Jimmy replied.

Half-Jimmy handed him the roll.

Jimmy tore off a sheet. Inserting it between his lips, Jimmy began to chew. When he had swallowed it, he tore off another, looked it over, and placed it in his mouth.

And so it continued.

As Jimmy's saliva ran out, he gripped the table, making the ungodly noises of a person scrubbing his throat with sandpaper.

Half-Jimmy stood by, pen and notebook in hand. Nervously, Half-Jimmy scribbled—the time, the people, the number of paper towels—all the while checking Jimmy to make sure he was okay.

Sweat gushed across Jimmy's face, the towels bulging in his mouth. Slowly the entire roll wiggled its way into his bowel.

Half-Jimmy hugged Jimmy. Jimmy belched.

"You've still got it, Jimmy," Half-Jimmy cried.

Half-Jimmy then pulled Jimmy toward a chair, making certain Jimmy was seated before checking his pulse.

Maria and I ran back to the other side of the room to report the scene to the girls. No one cared.

As the summer passed, we came to learn more of Jimmy.

As a child in rural Iowa, he was no different from the others until, one afternoon, walking home from school, he was struck by lightning. What Jimmy lost mentally, he made up for in other ways, including the ability to swallow paper towels. He also won an award for being the least lucky person in camp (he managed to find a dead dog in a cave and was struck again by lightning, this second time with no effect).

While other boys found Jimmy freakish, Half-Jimmy loved and encouraged him, becoming his nurse and biographer.

———

Toward the end of our final week at camp, our cabin counselor, Lauren, asked Maria and me if we wanted to join an overnight outing arranged by the camp. She assured us that we would love connecting with nature—something us city kids didn't do a lot. Nature to me meant roaches, squirrels, and rats. When we heard there was going to be free food, we agreed to go. Having to stick to a strict three-meals-a-day schedule was hard, so Maria and I spent many hours scheming about how to get more food.

Decked out in flip-flops, shorts, and tank tops, we waddled to the mess hall, where Lauren shoved two plastic bags into our arms.

"What is this?" Maria asked after peeking inside.

I looked inside my own bag. "One uncooked hot dog, and one apple," I announced.

"Camp!" Maria cursed.

Lauren ushered us to where the other kids were standing. They were dressed in down jackets and hiking shoes. My stomach started to turn.

"All right, survivalists," Lauren joked, "let's get moving. We have a long hike ahead of us."

She led us to the edge of camp where a tiny path snaked through the trees.

Maria and I lagged behind the group in our entirely unsuitable attire. Three hours later we entered a tiny clearing where the group stopped. Maria picked a splinter out of her heel.

In addition to courses on animal care (read dissection), the camp offered a class on wilderness survival. On the last weekend of camp, all the kids who took the class got to test their training on a trip to the woods. There were to be no s'mores, tents, or ghost stories. What Lauren had neglected to mention was that Maria and I had signed up for the survival weekend.

Lauren grinned. "Pair up!"

Maria and I started to look for more capable partners; the more capable partners started looking for anyone other than Maria and me.

The two of us were sent to the last clearing, where a girl with frizzy red hair and a camouflage bandanna and her burly partner were already setting up. Maria and I eyed each other warily.

Across the clearing campers were stacking branches to create teepees.

I nudged Maria. "We'd better start doing that."

Maria grudgingly agreed, and we started to collect and pile branches. An hour later the sun was nearing the horizon, and all we had was a small pile of twigs. I took some of the twigs and attempted to create a fire, while Maria worked on the teepee.

"I'm hungry," I whined.

"No surprise there," Maria retorted.

Nature tests even the best of friendships.

With no fire but something like a teepee, we huddled together and began to wolf down the uncooked weenies. The sun set. From the relative safety of our shelter, we watched the bandanna girl and her companion enjoy themselves in front of a roaring fire.

"How did they do it?" Maria hissed.

"Maybe it was something they learned in the survival class?" I replied.

Just then, we saw the stout girl reach into her backpack, grab a can of bug spray, and spray it into the fire. The fire blazed.

Maria looked troubled, something that could have been a side effect of the uncooked hot dogs.

"I don't think they should be doing that," she moaned, now clutching her stomach.

I nodded intelligently, making an effort to control my own bowels.

As Lauren made the rounds to check each campsite, we waved her over and reported on what the duo across the way were up to. Lauren immediately told them to pack their bags. She promptly called the camp to come pick them up. Maria and I sank further beneath our twigs. Bandanna girl and her partner glared in our direction, suspecting that it was us who'd ratted them out.

Our apprehension over what the two girls might do to us, combined with the ill and fragrant effects of the weenies, made me sweat. Maria was not faring any better. Crouching there, beneath the twigs of a dilapidated teepee, in desperate need of a bathroom, and fearing the wrath of those two girls, Maria and I started to laugh. Laugh and laugh and laugh.

What a pair we were. Two weenies.

AN UNEXPECTED JOURNEY

TOWARD THE END of seventh grade, there was to be an election for student president. A number of the most well liked and well known kids had declared their candidacies.

As the posters accumulated on the walls of the school, I was seized by this logic:

- popular kids, though liked by those in their own cliques, were often disliked, or even hated, by those in other groups;
- certain kids, like me, though popular with no one, were hated by no one; and
- if both of the above were true, then someone like me might get elected student council president.

Several days later it hit me: if "someone like me" might get elected student council president, then why not me?

I discussed it with my parents that evening. At first they were perplexed. My mom explained that to be on the student government, I would need to have friends who would vote for me. She immediately started to compose what she would say when I lost the election. My dad was taken aback by my newfound initiative, a trait which had skipped so many generations of Ripses that they hardly knew how to spell it.

The next day I announced my candidacy.

Of those who were running against me, and there were many, one was a portly, popular boy named Tim. Another, a Chinese American girl named Saijin. She had beautiful posters: "SAIJIN, It Rhymes with ASIAN." Not subtle, but likely effective in a school where half the students were Asian Americans.

My own candidacy was greeted with a strong lack of interest. Even the friends I had—my table—didn't support me, claiming that I couldn't win and that my candidacy would further humiliate us. In the days leading up to the election, candidates were supposed to describe our campaigns to the school. I had no slogans, no posters, no buttons, and the election was just weeks away.

Even Maria, my best friend, insisted that, out of fairness, she would have to give the other candidates a good look.

Toward the end of the campaign, a man who I did not recognize appeared at one of my parents' cocktail parties. He was sitting alone and had the expression on his face that I had when I was told I'd be sleeping next to the camp toilet.

He may have noticed me staring at him, for he waved me over.

"I am an old friend of your father's. And you are?"

"His daughter."

"Not entirely surprising, I suppose."

I headed in a different direction.

"It is a pleasure to meet you, sir, but I am running for class president and need to figure out how to get people to like me."

"Having trouble with that?"

"Since I was an infant."

"Where do you go to school?"

Suddenly I was deep into my school and what was happening with the election. Quite surprisingly, he listened.

At the end of my description of Tim, Saijin, and the other candidates, he announced, "Well, young lady, it sounds as if you are the best of a bad bunch."

The next day my posters went up at school:

"Nicolaia Rips, The Best of a Bad Bunch."

Students loved it.

After our final platform speeches in the cafeteria (mine was all about how we needed a water fountain on the fifth floor), I walked into the school, and there was a sign with the results of the election: "Nicolaia Rips—President."

This came as a surprise to everyone, and, yes, to me.

Once elected, I tried to carry out my campaign pledge, which was nothing more than giving kids a sense of what they have in common (and installing a water fountain). I tried to organize more dances and events so that kids from all cliques could be included. To be honest, it was difficult. As Karl Marx had offered, only the folks at the bottom yearn for equality. The popular kids could have cared less about my community outreach efforts. They already had each other. I did however manage to get that water fountain installed. It broke after a week but I fought hard to get it there. I may not have succeeded in schoolwide unity, but I did get my first taste of pointless educational bureaucracy.

One day, I asked my father about the man I'd met at the cocktail party.

"A good old friend," my father replied. "Brilliant fellow."

"But why haven't I met him before?"

"He was just released from prison."

"What was he in for?"

"Smuggling antiquities or something like that. I don't know all the details."

I glanced at the collection of terra-cotta figures on top of our bookshelves.

"How does he support himself now that he's out of prison?"

"Gin and tonics."

MY INTERESTED LOOK

I PASSED THE final few weeks of seventh grade sitting in the Stoner Corner next to Joseph (Greta's boyfriend). By this point in the year, teachers had given up trying to educate us and were content to sit back as we conversed quietly. One afternoon, Joseph and I had just finished a game of tic-tac-toe, and he was filling me in on the latest school gossip.

He was going on about how Hunter had been asked out by the prettiest girl in the school (Penelope Brewster) and how he had rejected her. This piece of news was very interesting since I'd always had a bit of a thing for Hunter.

Though I was eager to hear more, Joseph stopped and refused to continue. When I pressed him, he remarked that I obviously wasn't interested in what he was saying. I was dumbstruck.

"Me? Not interested! How could you think that?!"

"You look bored—you've got the expression my grandfather has on his face after he falls asleep but before his dentures slide out of his mouth."

What was this?

I'd assumed that when I was interested in something I showed it.

A day or so later, I was at a piano recital, organized and filmed by an actor whom my parents knew from the Chelsea. There were about fifty people.

The piano player, a man in his eighties, had been a child sensation but, owing to stage fright, no longer played publicly. My parents' friend, the actor, had met the piano player and become intrigued by him. Soon the actor made it his mission to coax the pianist back on stage. The concert that evening was the pianist's first in fifty-five years.

The actor began the evening by telling the story of the pianist. But the actor also spoke of his own difficulties: he'd begun acting as a child, achieved great success in his twenties and thirties, but was now worried about his future.

I was in awe of what I was listening to. The actor was both brave and humble.

"Nicki?"

Me?

"Nicki?"

No doubt about it. The actor was staring at me from the podium and calling my name.

"How old are you?" he asked.

"Thirteen."

I was confused by his question since he knew exactly how old I was. I was the same age as his daughter, one of my oldest family friends. But he was smart and I imagined he was using the question as a lead into something like:

"I was exactly Nicki's age when I started acting. At first it was difficult. I had to struggle to learn how to act. People thought that only sissies acted, and kids made fun of me. When I look at Nicki, I feel the need to tell her that whatever fears she may have along the way, she will one day be a great success."

Instead, he announced to the audience:

"As soon as I started telling you about my midlife crisis, Nicki got bored."

The audience laughed.

I was embarrassed. And confused. Why did he think I was bored? I had on my interested face!

I buried my head in my mother's shoulder as the cameras zoomed in on me. As the crowd's laughter died down, Mom whispered, "It's true, as soon as he started talking about his life your face went slack."

The following morning, Father joked about what had happened at the recital.

I returned to sobbing.

"I wasn't trying to insult your friend," I told him (sob, sob), "that's just how I look when I'm interested!"

"Well, my daughter, you're just going to have to find a new look."

In the following weeks I tried various expressions. To get the faces down, I would imagine myself in a various interesting situations. There was "walking past a man leading his cat on a leash" interest and "my dad just found another West African dung sculpture" interest, "Penelope Brewster was wearing a thong today" interest and "my uncle is a right-wing Republican" interest. When I thought I had one of the faces right, I would photograph myself and show the photo to my mom.

I had a great time with this, and by the end of the week, I had a number of interested faces. All of them, I must admit, were convincing.

I decided that I would try them out on Joseph. He could be counted on for an honest opinion.

Later that day, Joseph was rambling on about his grand-father, who lived with Joseph and, more significantly, shared a bathroom with him.

According to Joseph, his grandfather had been consti-pated for three decades (a condition he blamed on his late wife's brisket), but had recently come up with a mixture of tea leaves, black pepper, and Maalox, which, he claimed, had cured him.

As Joseph talked, I knew that I was wearing the right face, for Joseph, interpreting my look as one of interest

(with a dash of revulsion), dove into ever greater details of what he had learned of his grandfather's digestive tract. The work I had done over the last months was paying off.

CINDERELLA

I CAN'T DENY that before I ran for president of my eighth-grade class, it had occurred to me that if I was elected, I'd be in a position to arrange events that would give me an excuse to meet the boys at school.

So the first thing that I decided to do in my new position was to organize a dance, a Halloween dance. I picked Hallow-een because it continued to be my favorite holiday. I wanted to do something fun and scary—like the inspired foolery that I'd grown up with at the hotel.

The dance also provided me with the opportunity to approach boys I liked and ask them to help out with refresh-ments, music, decorations, and tickets. By the time the big night rolled around, the boys and I would be friends and they would ask me to dance. At least that was the plan. Even if this failed, everyone would be in disguise (I as Cinderella), and the boys might just confuse me for one of the attractive girls.

I'd given out the assignments days in advance. Arriving at

school in the late afternoon, I waited in the cafeteria for the boys to arrive and make good on their promises.

An hour before the dance, when no one had appeared, I placed some calls. Of those few boys I was able to reach by phone, all showed a frightening nonchalance about their tasks. I attempted to be nonchalant about their nonchalance. It didn't work.

Thirty minutes before the dance, nothing was ready. With little time, I managed to pull together some decorations and set up some tables. One of the boys had dropped off a bowl of bean dip which, he assured me, was what "Grandma made for Mom's senior prom." From the look of the dip, it wasn't clear whether this was a cryogenically preserved bowl of what Granny had made decades earlier or something fresher. I put the dip on the table and sat down.

Exhausted, I still needed to change into my costume when Meredith Penny, the parent in charge of the dance (of course), arrived.

She began to shout commands.

"The floor in the main hall—sweep it! And the windows, clean them! And the curtain on the stage, fix it . . ."

I interrupted.

"But I need time to get into my costume."

"Then work faster."

I worked faster than I'd ever worked in my life, and with five minutes to spare, I rushed toward the lockers. But hefty

Meredith blocked my path. She pointed to the table with the dip and drink. No one was there to serve them.

I made my way to the table, still sweating from my tasks. After an hour or two, with everyone but me enjoying themselves, I noticed a commotion at the center of the dance floor. In all the running around to prepare, I'd neglected to make certain that someone was supervising the Licker, who, disguised as Captain Crunch, was able to advance on people who otherwise would have stayed far away.

I had no time to make sure that the Licker stayed out of trouble, so there was only one thing to do. I asked him if he would do me the favor of retrieving an item from the janitor's closet down the hall from the cafeteria. Once the Licker was inside, I closed the door.

That taken care of, I returned to a list of assignments which Meredith had taped to my chair. I raced over to the snack table.

Pressing my overheated noggin against the side of the frosty dip, I watched as others (including the boys who had neglected the jobs I'd given them) arrived. I felt like Cinderella if Cinderella's fairy godmother had never shown up.

Before leaving the dance, Meredith had made certain that the list was so long that I would have little chance to dance and that I would be in that awful cafeteria, taking down decorations and throwing away garbage, until well after everyone else had left. And I was already exhausted.

If I needed a reason to feel sorry for myself, this was it.

My only comfort was that with Meredith's departure, things couldn't get worse.

Then they did.

Through the rear doors of the cafeteria came a group of parents, all dressed in costume. Meredith, who had never actually left, led the way. Accompanying her, against its will, was Meredith's reawakened pleather costume, which had, decades before, shocked the citizens of Pagosa Springs.

"Who's That Girl," Meredith's favorite, was on the speakers.

"When you see her, say a prayer and kiss your heart goodbye. She's trouble, in a word . . ."

As Meredith drew closer to me and the dip, I was able to make out the details of her outfit: black pleather tights, pointy pleather bra, teased hair, and a long metal chain around her neck.

Given her girth, upward-thrusting bra, black makeup, and chain swinging back and forth across her torso, the dancing Meredith resembled a battleship that had been struck by enemy fire and was listing badly.

As kids fled, I knew that my Halloween dance was over and would soon be known as the biggest catastrophe in the history of our middle school. But that was its fate: it had been organized by the school idiot.

At that instant the music stopped.

"Meredith, get off the floor!"

The voice came loudly from the opposite side of the auditorium.

"This is *our* dance."

Meredith's eyes searched violently for her antagonist.

Hunter Whiting, the best-looking boy in the school, stepped forward.

"You heard it, Meredith. GET OFF THE FLOOR."

To everyone's amazement, Meredith Penny, without a word, left the floor, left the auditorium, and left our future. Never had so much material girl disappeared so quickly.

But Hunter was not through.

"Now I want to say something that should have been said a long time ago. There is someone who has been working very, very hard so that we can enjoy ourselves. And it is about time that we thanked that person, someone who is not only hard-working and modest but also the prettiest girl I know."

He turned to the table where I was sitting.

Me?

Hunter grinned.

I stood up. I felt the top of my head, my black curls still tucked neatly behind a tiara.

No one was laughing.

I walked from behind the table. A waltz came on.

Others began to sway. And when I was within reach of Hunter, he held out his hand. I took it, placing my other hand on his shoulder. He reached his arm around my waist and pulled me close. So close I could smell his Axe body spray. (One of the girls at school had given all the cute boys a can of Axe, so our school permanently smelled of perfume and sweat.)

"Hunter," I sighed.

He brushed a strand of hair that had fallen from my tiara.

And then we danced, Hunter holding me in his caring though muscular arms as the music carried us around the room.

"It's as if there's no one else in the room," he whispered.

"I know . . ." I replied, my eyes closed, my face pressed against his shoulder.

"And you have dip in your hair."

What?

"I said there's dip below your face, and if you don't get up your head's going in."

I opened my eyes. The dip was looming under me, the Licker just above. As I fell asleep my head had lolled closer and closer to the ominous bowl, hovering just above.

"I'm sorry but someone locked me in the closet, and I just got out." He shrugged. "Worse things have happened. I came here, and everyone was gone. Except you, taking a nap."

I was too shocked not to ask.

"Hunter?"

"He's gone with the others."

"Did we dance?" I asked.

The Licker paused. He liked me too much to tell me the truth.

"Here, let me help you clean up," he offered.

With that he began gathering trash off the tables and floor.

He did not look back at me, allowing me time to adjust to what had never happened.

When we finished cleaning the gymnasium, he approached me. In his hand was a small plastic bag. It was the one I'd brought to the dance. Still inside were my golden gown, matching slippers, and tiara.

It was late at night, and no one was on the street. We walked each other to the corner and said good night.

THE BANANA PEELS OF OPTIMISM

LUNCH AT TABLE 17 was a time usually devoted to bemoaning various embarrassing social situations. One day I found myself the focus of everyone at my table's gaze.

"Where do you want to go?"

This came from Maria and was a question echoed by every kid in my school. And we would not stop asking it for the next few months, each time more nervously. Maria, luckily, got to opt out of the entire process because her family was moving back to Italy.

Typical of my parents, they had done nothing to figure out where I should go to high school, so I took the elevator down to the lobby of the Chelsea, hoping that someone there had gone to high school in New York and would know what was going on.

It was late in the afternoon and I caught the Crafties in the window of sobriety between lunch and predinner cocktails at El Quijote. I emptied my sack of complaints.

223

Waving his cane to silence the others, Mr. Crafty began.

"As I look back on my life, the people I met at Hotchkiss and then the Naval Academy helped me to achieve my greatest accomplishments. Am I proud to admit that? No, but the advantage cannot be denied."

"Excuse me," interrupted Uber-Crafty, "you never went to Hotchkiss, and it was the Capitan, not you, who went to the Naval Academy."

"Well, what about 'my greatest accomplishments'?" asked Mr. Crafty, surprised at the revision to his biography.

"Locked securely in the future."

"Funny man, but let me remind you"—Mr. Crafty now had the end of his cane stuck in Uber-Crafty's chest—"'the distinction between the past, present, and future is only a persistent illusion.'"

"Who said that, Mr. Crafty?" I questioned.

"I can assure you that he doesn't remember," Uber-Crafty responded. "The point that he is trying to make is that if you want to get into a good college you will need to attend a private high school."

This was the first I'd heard of such a thing. Noting my surprise, Uber-Crafty continued.

"Over half the kids from private schools in this city go to good colleges, even if they're screw-ups. That's not true of public schools."

I was beginning to feel a fever coming on.

"Loaded parents know that the best way to get their lit-

them suffer and die; a place where one could spend years alone and not understand why; not an easy place, an often painful place.

———

The whole problem of what to perform for my audition was made easier when I discovered a list of suggested monologues on the LaGuardia website. When I presented the list to my parents, my mother suggested I do the Auntie Mame monologue that I'd been performing at cocktail parties since I was five.

"It's a sure win!" she said.

But my father disagreed. He couldn't believe that I would even consider doing a monologue from the school's list. Why, he asked, bore the judges with something they'd heard a thousand times?

With that he set off to find the right monologue.

And find it he did. After searching through the theater section in our local library, he reappeared with a couple of handwritten pages which he had copied out of a book.

In the passage my father gave me, a teenage girl attempts to tell her family about something amusing she'd seen on *Oprah*—an interview Oprah had done with twin sisters. The parents of the girl aren't listening, choosing instead to shout at each other. Frustrated by being ignored, the girl's description of the interview becomes more and more manic.

It seemed funny to me, and Father's argument about boring the judges with things they'd already heard made a certain amount of sense. Then again, most of what my father said had a small amount of sense packed inside it. The bait in the bear trap.

At the last minute, I decided that I would also apply to the voice studio. Choosing a song was much easier. My godfather, who had a career in musical theater, introduced me to a song that Carol Burnett had performed on Broadway when she was a young woman. The song was "Shy" and I loved it, as I loved everything that Carol Burnett sang.

An advantage of the song was that no one else was going to perform it. The girls who were applying to LaGuardia were more likely to sing something contemporary, like a song by Taylor Swift or Adele.

On the day of the audition, my parents accompanied me to LaGuardia. The audition was at 8:00 in the morning. Leaving the subway on Sixty-fifth street, we walked the several blocks to the school. I began to go over what I'd prepared for the audition, but I didn't get very far, for we were immediately interrupted by other kids, with other parents, moving in the same direction. As we approached the building, we ran into a wall of kids who had arrived well before us and had already formed a line which, beginning at the school, ran around the block.

"Twenty thousand," one of the students whispered to me as I took my place in line.

I shook.

them suffer and die; a place where one could spend years alone and not understand why; not an easy place, an often painful place.

———

The whole problem of what to perform for my audition was made easier when I discovered a list of suggested monologues on the LaGuardia website. When I presented the list to my parents, my mother suggested I do the Auntie Mame monologue that I'd been performing at cocktail parties since I was five.

"It's a sure win!" she said.

But my father disagreed. He couldn't believe that I would even consider doing a monologue from the school's list. Why, he asked, bore the judges with something they'd heard a thousand times?

With that he set off to find the right monologue.

And find it he did. After searching through the theater section in our local library, he reappeared with a couple of handwritten pages which he had copied out of a book.

In the passage my father gave me, a teenage girl attempts to tell her family about something amusing she'd seen on *Oprah*—an interview Oprah had done with twin sisters. The parents of the girl aren't listening, choosing instead to shout at each other. Frustrated by being ignored, the girl's description of the interview becomes more and more manic.

It seemed funny to me, and Father's argument about boring the judges with things they'd already heard made a certain amount of sense. Then again, most of what my father said had a small amount of sense packed inside it. The bait in the bear trap.

At the last minute, I decided that I would also apply to the voice studio. Choosing a song was much easier. My godfather, who had a career in musical theater, introduced me to a song that Carol Burnett had performed on Broadway when she was a young woman. The song was "Shy" and I loved it, as I loved everything that Carol Burnett sang.

An advantage of the song was that no one else was going to perform it. The girls who were applying to LaGuardia were more likely to sing something contemporary, like a song by Taylor Swift or Adele.

On the day of the audition, my parents accompanied me to LaGuardia. The audition was at 8:00 in the morning. Leaving the subway on Sixty-fifth street, we walked the several blocks to the school. I began to go over what I'd prepared for the audition, but I didn't get very far, for we were immediately interrupted by other kids, with other parents, moving in the same direction. As we approached the building, we ran into a wall of kids who had arrived well before us and had already formed a line which, beginning at the school, ran around the block.

"Twenty thousand," one of the students whispered to me as I took my place in line.

I shook.

Directly in front of me was a short boy with dreadlocks. He was wearing a black suit and white shirt. His tie was poorly knotted and his cuffs frayed. He had no parents with him. Under his arm was a portfolio of drawings.

Two kids in front of him was a girl whose grandfather's name was embossed on a building down the street.

Never before had I seen so many kids from so many different parts of New York. Each of us would be required to perform, and if the judges were interested, we would be called back for another performance and interview.

But the important thing was the performance, and for that, it did not matter who you were or where you came from. The idea was thrilling and terrifying.

I glanced at my parents. If I was not mistaken, it was the first time I saw a dent in their optimism.

I, on the other hand, had been prepared for the worst but this exceeded my greatest fears. And isn't that the hellish thing about life: there is only underestimating the worst.

An hour and a half later, I was inside.

My first audition was for the vocal studio. I sat in the long line of chairs outside the auditorium. I had gone over the song many times, and I knew it. I also reminded myself that Mom had a beautiful voice and that, if I had inherited just part of it, I had a shot.

As I drew closer to the door of the auditorium, I could hear the other students performing. Each voice seemed better than the last, and the first was better than mine. But there was one thing that I had and they didn't: while they all performed the same pop songs, I would be performing an ancient gem, "Shy."

I was now sitting right outside the auditorium. The girl before me—a thin young girl with a quiet manner—had just walked in. She began, as all others had, by introducing her song.

"Today," she announced, "I shall sing a song by Mary Rogers . . ."

What, what?

"Written in 1958 . . ."

Wait a minute . . .

"Titled . . ."

It couldn't be . . .

"'Shy.'"

No!

She began. And within a few stanzas, you'd have thought Ethel Merman had bolted from her grave. The room shook with this girl's voice. And with the room shaking and my mind spinning, I was unable to get to my feet fast enough to run out of the school.

My name was called. I had no choice but to march into the room and keep my chin up.

On the plus side, I got through it. Though there was a spark of snickering from the judges at the beginning, this was quickly doused by disinterest.

As I left the auditorium, filing past the others who were

waiting for their chance to sing, I wondered how many of them were going to sing "Shy" or something like it. How many of them were like me: kids who others considered weird, backward, and unlikable? And was this possibly, just possibly, a school for such characters?

But I didn't have much time to think about this. There was still the audition for the acting studio. I rushed to the basement, where three judges waited for me in a small classroom.

When I announced the name of the play, two of the judges leaned forward. Obviously no one had performed it, let alone the student just before me. A good start.

The attention of the three judges did not move from me, and as soon as I'd finished, they began talking among themselves with energy. Seeing that the discussion needed more time, they asked me to step outside. This could only be a good sign.

Upon being called back into the room, they asked if I would answer a few questions. Of course. I was feeling confident. I'd heard that acceptance notices would not be sent out for another couple months, but perhaps they made exceptions for the especially talented.

"Do you know anything about the play you performed?" was their first question.

My father, you will remember, had only given me a couple pages he'd copied from a book, but he'd given me enough of a description of the rest of the play for me to take a shot at an answer.

"The main character, my character," I began, "is a young woman . . ."

But that was as far as I was going to get.

"A young woman? Are you certain?"

There was a click in those words—the sound of a safety being flipped off a rifle.

"A young*ish* woman . . ." I sputtered.

"It's my recollection," a judge interrupted, "that she was forty."

"The new fourteen?" I tried.

Not a chuckle. I was now in their crosshairs.

"For your information, Miss Rips"—this from one of the two judges who'd perked up when I'd mentioned the name of the play—"there is little funny about the play: the protagonist just had a miscarriage and is an alcoholic—the result of having married a Jewish man whose family hates her because she's Christian."

Father! my mind screamed.

Now it made sense. He had only given me a couple pages of the play because he knew that if I'd read the whole thing, it would be clear to me that the role was not for a thirteen-year-old girl.

But it was my fault. Why had I listened to him? For that matter, why had I ever listened to him? He nearly murdered my first crush, caused me to be diagnosed with an eye disorder, and initiated countless other failed schemes and misadventures.

"And those sisters you were making fun of in your monologue were Siamese twins," the same judge added.

So the play was not only inappropriate for my age but was politically incorrect, and that, at a public high school in New York, was inexcusable.

"Pardon me," I managed. "Are we finished?"

I should have seen the whole thing coming. What had possessed me to think I could go anywhere near this school? I could blame my father but, honestly, it was my delusion which led me to the auditions in the first place.

I was a fool.

THE PLAYING FIELDS
OF WEST CHELSEA

I VOWED THAT before I left middle school, I would get myself invited to one of the soccer games that the popular kids spent their afternoons playing.

The key to that invitation was Joseph, my Stoner Corner companion.

A good-looking boy, Joseph was unusually lazy. While others as popular as Joseph spent their time making fun of kids like me, Joseph decided that making fun of others took too much energy.

Joseph was lethargic, but you'd think he would have bothered to learn a thing or two about his own anatomy; evidently not, since one day in health class, upon being questioned by our teacher on some special part of the male body, he sat shocked, and glanced toward me for the answer.

The question was how many "gonads" do boys have.

I felt sorry for Joseph and whispered my best guess.

Wrong.

That did not stop good-natured Joseph from thanking me for trying to help him, and I knew that he was the sort who would return the favor.

So just weeks before school ended, Joseph and I strolled onto the soccer field in west Chelsea together.

In addition to the pretty boys, there was the usual crowd of attractive female onlookers: Penelope Brewster, Ana Penny, and Greta (who by then had dumped Joseph).

But there was someone else there that day . . . the Schnoz.

The Schnoz hadn't been included because he was well liked (he was too odd for that and, of course, there was the whole problem with the slootz), but because he was from Europe and knew how to play soccer.

After nodding to the Schnoz, I joined the girls on the sidelines. They appeared to accept my arrival as some sort of strange end-of-middle-school doomsday situation and continued on with their conversation about high schools. Acceptance letters would arrive any day and it was all anyone could talk about.

Just before the game was to start, I spotted a speck moving across the field. As the speck drew closer, it remained a speck, defying the laws of optics until immediately before us. It was none other than my first crush—Uhura.

My presence at this event was so unlikely that Uhura walked right up to our group and greeted his friends without realizing I was there.

In case any of us had forgotten that he was smart, he announced how well he had done on the test to get into what was said to be the best school for science and mathematics in the city. This was especially bothersome to me because I was facing certain refusal at the only school I applied to.

"It couldn't hurt," I pointed out, "that you were named after the communications officer of a starship."

Noticing me, he flinched. I'd infiltrated his lair, and he wasn't pleased.

He turned to Penelope Brewster.

"My girlfriend wanted you to know that she's sorry she couldn't make it today. Her family is on the Island."

The point here was that her family was rich.

"Staten Island?" I asked innocently.

"No," he snapped. "The Hamptons."

I was about to release my most dismissive "The Hamptons, Uhura? Really?" when the Schnoz bolted toward us. The game was about to start, and he saw this as his last chance to win back the affection of the girls who once adored him.

"Helloooo, slootz!"

Uhura glared at the Schnoz, offended by the interruption.

"Today I show you slootz something special," the Schnoz announced, taking no notice of Uhura.

Uhura, who had been staring at the Schnoz, was now focused on me, his sneer replaced with something else. It looked a little bit like respect.

But why?

Then it came to me. Uhura thought the Schnoz was my boyfriend.

And why wouldn't he think that: in my last conversation with Uhura, I'd assembled a Build-a-Boyfriend which looked a lot like the Schnoz—tall, beautiful, and foreign.

Now I was torn. On one hand, the appearance of the Schnoz would convince Uhura that I had a boyfriend and wasn't stalking him. On the other hand . . . well, I'm not so sure what the other hand was, but there had to be something.

I was going through the possibilities when I noticed that everyone, including Uhura, was staring at the Schnoz.

Just in back of me, the Schnoz had flipped himself upside down. Supported by his hands and the top of his head, he stretched his legs straight upward.

From there, slowly, slowly, he brought his legs down until they were perpendicular to his body. A human right angle.

And in this position he remained until, suddenly, he jerked his knees toward his torso.

Straightening his legs out again, he repeated the contraction. This he did two more times and then . . .

Kaboom.

His head buried in the grass, he cried out to the girls:

"I fart. You smell!"

Releasing one of his arms, he waved his hand around his buttocks.

"You smell. I fart."

Another jerk of his legs.

Kaboom.

"I fart again. You smell again! *Sì,* slootz?!"

He laughed maniacally.

Uhura was standing within inches of the Schnoz and received the worst of it. As he reeled, the Schnoz used his legs to scissor Uhura's head, drawing it into his crotch.

Racing away, we looked back at Uhura. There was no saving him.

Uhura took the final blast to the face.

From then on, I had no desire to see Uhura, his image forever attached to the carnage of that afternoon. I was cured of Uhura as he was cured in the fumes of the Schnoz.

MR. CRAFTY MOVES OUT

COMING HOME FROM school one day I noticed that Mr. Crafty's seat in the lobby was without Mr. Crafty. My first thought was that he'd had another stroke and was in the hospital or worse. I asked the woman behind the front desk where he had gone, but she had no idea.

If there was anyone who had the answer, it would be Uber-Crafty, his best friend, who lived on the fifth floor. I ran up to his apartment. He was there, painting, and wasn't pleased to be interrupted. But he invited me in.

His apartment was so full of paintings that there was nowhere to sit. Everything but his bed and his canvases had been cleared out. I stood in front of a brightly painted nude girl whose head was turned on its side, resting atop her own shoulder. The first layer of the canvas was thousands of postage stamps.

But I was not there to admire his work. He knew that. Mr. Crafty, he told me, had left the hotel and would not return.

Mr. Crafty had received a call from a woman who claimed to have been a friend of his from high school. He didn't recognize her name.

They arranged to meet in the lobby of the hotel, and when they did, he remembered that this woman was someone with whom he had once been very much in love. As Mr. Crafty's story spread further into his past, he was awakening things in himself. And on that day, he got up out of his chair, walked slowly out the front door of the hotel, and never returned, leaving his friends forever, including his best friend, Uber-Crafty.

It was rumored that the woman lived in a beautiful home in Connecticut, where she would care for Mr. Crafty and help him to overcome his paralysis.

I asked Uber-Crafty how he felt about all that had happened with his friend. Uber-Crafty smiled and delivered the ultimate declaration of respect and affection.

"Crafty."

I would like to think that Mr. Crafty knew, on some subconscious level, that memories are not linear or static, but overlapping, twisting, and dynamic. And that one needs to add the fuel of new memories to keep the whole thing churning. I believe that Mr. Crafty left to create his own memories, but that he took some of the Capitan, Uber-Crafty, Crafty One and Two and, hopefully, me with him.

AT LAST

WE KNEW IT was coming. But not like this.

Let me take a step back.

There is a period between the application deadlines for high school and the arrival of acceptance letters. That period is long enough to allow tensions to subside, and there is a general sense of good feeling. Even one's enemies seem to lose their bite.

It was in this atmosphere that we were enjoying ourselves when an announcement was made on the loudspeaker that we had to report to the cafeteria immediately. The cafeteria doubled as the gymnasium, and after lunch, the tables were pushed aside, the basketball hoops lowered, and various gymnastic equipment returned

Around three o'clock the sweat from the athletes mixed with the odor of cooked vegetables and luncheon meats.

It was in this environment that the principal had gathered us. With the temperature outside above 80 degrees and the room now stuffed, we felt nauseous.

"Students," the principal began, "when I say your name, raise your hand."

As the principal called our names, the vice principal walked into the crowd of kids and handed each of us an envelope. Was this part of our graduation? Our diplomas?

Then a cry. A cry sharp and slicing. The world came crashing down on Atlas's feet: it was not our diplomas; not even our report cards. It was our high school acceptance letters.

Nothing could have been crueler. Instead of allowing us to absorb our disappointment alone, in our homes, with our families, we were being outed in front of every other kid in the school.

The wailing began immediately. Followed by cursing. The few who'd been accepted to their schools of choice were sensitive enough to keep quiet, so the dominant sound was of inflating pain.

But word of those with good news could not be suppressed, and onto the bonfire of disappointment was tossed the gasoline of jealousy.

Some kids yelled at each other, others pounded their fists against the walls. But no one wanted to leave the room. We were the battered fighters who insisted on staying in the ring, eyes swollen, mouths filled with blood, until the end.

I didn't know what to do. The principal was still at the start of the alphabet, so I had time to think. I wanted to avoid the suffering. Then I remembered a promise I'd made months before: my mother had made me swear that I would not open my envelope until she was with me.

My mother has great intuition, especially when it comes to me. She is also my greatest comfort. Though I told her that I was prepared for rejection, she knew me, understanding that it would be hard on me, and she also understood that at that moment, I would want her to be there.

When my name was called, I took my envelope and, with the greatest will I'd ever mustered, stuffed it into my pocket and marched out of the school, my fingers plugged into my ears.

Outside, I stood alone, the sun brushed my face. I pulled out my phone and dialed my mother. She didn't pick up. I tried again. No answer. I left the message that I'd received my high school letter and I was heading home.

By now, kids were leaving the school. I spotted Maria, the Planker, and others from my table huddled on a corner, all of them talking about their letters.

When they heard that I hadn't opened mine, they couldn't believe it. They thought that by calling my mother and leaving a message, I'd satisfied my promise. But it was not so much the pledge to my mother. I didn't want them to see my disappointment. There was also the suspicion that they might not be as sympathetic as I would want them to be.

We walked another few yards.

It was too much for Maria. She lunged at me.

"OPEN THE DAMN LETTER!"

She grabbed the letter from my pocket, and I, trying to get it back, lost my balance, knocking both of us over.

The Planker, shaking his head, stared at us on the gum-speckled pavement. Meanwhile the letter floated into the middle of the road, where Krysta, the crossing guard, grabbed it. Halting traffic, she held it up, slowly turning it over in her hands.

As she returned to the sidewalk, to the soundtrack of honks and cursing, she opened the letter.

I gasped. Maria helped me to my feet.

Krysta frowned.

"You're going to LaGuardia."

———

Walking back to the hotel, I thought about my mom. She was the one who was always surprising me with good news; now I had something for her.

As I entered the lobby, Uber-Crafty and Crafty Two were in their chairs. Stormé was there. I nodded to them, but wasn't going to stop. I needed to get upstairs to Mom.

"Excuse me."

It was Uber-Crafty.

"Where are you going?"

Puzzled, I turned toward him.

"Did you forget to tell us something, Little Crafty?"

Was it that obvious? Did they know me that well?

It was too much to think about.

But think about it I did. Their faces, their gestures, their personalities, their humor, and their kindness had carried me through, unaware.

When I told them about LaGuardia, they were on their feet hugging me.

―――――

The next day, Maria, the Planker, Joshua, the Licker, and I met up at a coffee shop in the Village. We were there as we had been so many times in the years before. And, as so many times before, a couple tables away were the popular kids from our school. The ones I'd spent so much of my life pursuing.

All of us knew that the next few months could be our last opportunity to spend so much time together. We might see each other in passing, but that would be it. Shortly we would be going off without each other. Off to new schools, new lives.

Whether it was from the weight of this or something else that none of us could articulate, the Planker stood up, moved his chair aside, and, in the space where his chair had been, lay facedown on the floor.

Immediately the kids from the other table began to point and laugh, making sure that no one else in the coffee shop missed the Planker.

As the laughter in the room rose, I knew exactly what I needed to do.

I stood up, moved my chair over, and lay down next to him. Staring up from the floor, the world, for the very first time in my life, could not have looked better.

AUTHOR'S NOTE

AS A CHILD, I would return home each afternoon and lament to my parents about my tragedies: the malignant odor that emanated from the locker rooms, my daily social faux pas, and my deafening loneliness. Upon my arrival in middle school, my father, bored by my complaints, told me to "write it down," which I did. As I wrote, I would ask my parents to tell me what I couldn't know. As we talked, my stories became richer, more amusing, less painful than what I experienced. Toward the end of eighth grade, I presented my English teacher with a bound-up copy of my journal as my end-of-year project. She asked me if I would read one of the stories at my graduation. My parents were shocked—not so much at the story as at the initiative it took to produce the journal, initiative being a trait which, as my father explained it, had skipped so many generations of his family that they hardly knew how to spell it. For the past three years, I have been working with my father to flesh out my stories. He has guided me, teaching me how to structure a story, weave together themes, and connect loose ends into a narrative. For this reason, the book is a unique effort between a father and a daughter. These stories have evolved with each year, expanding as I have, going back and forth between the two of us as we sat in cafés over the weekends. I know my teachers and classmates and others will not recognize some of the events that I recount, any more than they will recognize their names, which have been changed. Nor should they, because these are the stories of my life; stories that are remembered, imagined, passed down, and often a combination. They are as legitimate as my memories, which are fallible and mysterious, and as real as you care to believe.

ACKNOWLEDGMENTS

HERE ARE PEOPLE who, despite my age (and lack of maturity), took me and this project seriously. For this, they have been punished by having to help with the book, and help they did:

I would like to thank my incredible editor, Liese Mayer, whose persistence and intuition turned this into something readable; my agents, Nicole Aragi and Duvall Osteen, whose dedication to this book has been both mystifying and wonderful; the entire marketing and publicity team at Scribner, who taught me more about the habits of my generation then I ever knew; and Nan Graham, whose powerful presence behind this book took it to publication.

Accolades go out to the readers and editors Alex Traub and Paulina Porizkova, who had the bad luck of being the first to get ahold of it, but whose insights made it so much more for everyone who read it after.

Thanks to my parents, without whose genetic material I would be sorely disadvantaged. Thank you, mom, for sticking up for me when I need it. Your ceaseless optimism, love, and graciousness is a lesson. As to my magical father, who spins words into worlds, I have been privileged to have grown up with him and been privy to his mind. Thank you for being my role model and teacher.

Thanks to my high school friends, who are a phenomenal support system. If I had known you guys in elementary school, this book would never have been written.

Lastly, I am eternally in debt to my middle school teacher Ms. Boyd, who read this back in its first stages and saw something that she encouraged, pushing me to make more of it. Thank you.